If you are married, read this book. If you are not yet married, read this book (it will help you prepare for this most important relationship). If you have been married and are no longer, read this book (it can help you mend that relationship and gain perspective and healing). Unless you live on a deserted island, read this book! Ministry can be brutal on relationships and down time hard to come by...Tom and Sandi share their deeply personal wounds, growth areas, and victories so that we can learn from the work that the Lord is doing in their marriage. Their authenticity shines through each page. If you don't know Tom or Sandi personally, you will feel like you do by the time you finish this great tool. Just read it.

~ Sue Nellis, pastor

This is a book that should be in the hands of every ministry couple. Convicting, penetrating, engaging, transparent. Tom and Sandi share their personal story and struggles in a way that draws you in and shows you the way. The challenges they faced in their marriage are familiar to every couple who carry the weight of ministry. It is a must read for those who balance the daily realities of marriage and ministry. Thank you Blaylock's for your passion for marriage and ministry and your willingness to be vulnerable.

~ Bill Lepley, pastor

Tom and Sandi open up about their struggles in ministry in a very straightforward way. The writing is refreshing and keeps your interest. Having both Tom and Sandi writing sections of the book brings a wonderful clarity to the way they worked through the struggles and emerged a far healthier and happy couple. The book presents many good ideas for strengthening the marriage relationship and getting back on track in living out our mission to make disciples together. Many of you will find this book very helpful, especially those struggling with balancing church planting, marriage and family.

~ Dr. Dan Riemenschneider, Director of Strengthening Local Churches for the Missionary Church

Marriage on Mission

How strengthening your marriage
multiplies your missional impact

Tom and Sandi Blaylock

MARRIAGE *on* MISSION
MINISTRIES

Dedication

We dedicate this book to our dear friends
Dana and Jimmy Gretzinger.
Your passion for God and love for one another
draw us in to the adventure of a marriage on mission.

Contents

Foreword

When a friend asks you to review their book, it is a moment that brings a bit of tension, because until you read it you can't be sure if you will be able to give an enthusiastic endorsement.

But when I sat down to read the Blaylocks' new book, *Marriage on Mission*, I realized very quickly how easy it was going to be to recommend their book!

Tom and Sandi have written a warm, personal and amazingly accessible account of the realities that we often face when marriage and ministry walk together.

Instead of the usual book that focuses on statistics and trends to make the case that marriages are in trouble, *Marriage on Mission* plunges the reader into the real-life story of Tom and Sandi's marriage as it unfolded.

Their vulnerable retelling of their darkest days is so well written that you feel a sense of rising tension as their marriage begins a slow arc toward disaster like a car sliding sideways on ice.

Each chapter combines realistic dialogue, honest narrative and practical, hard-earned wisdom in memorable principles.

Many will find that the first chapter alone is worth the price of the book as the Blaylocks explain the difficulties they faced at the realization that Sandi is an external processor of her feelings, while Tom is an internal processor. The many quotations from their journals from those days serve to draw you in to the scene until you feel that you are watching the events unfold in real time.

Every chapter adds another layer of insight and wisdom to this task that we share... serving the Lord in the everyday pressures of ministry while wrestling with the best ways to strengthen and stabilize our marriages and families in the process.

I can tell you after watching Tom and Sandi for years, that they love Jesus passionately, and that they are deeply and lovingly committed to each other.

As their friends, Sue and I can testify to their authentic faith, their unshakable commitment to their marriage, and their vulnerability as they have taken this journey together.

I highly recommend this book to anyone in ministry. While every marriage is different, I believe you will see your reflection somewhere in the pages of this book.

The Blaylocks have written "the book" on marriage in ministry. They have respected the reader enough to avoid superficial solutions or shallow conclusions. And it is obvious they have respected each other deeply in the process of telling their story.

I will be recommending their book to all of our pastors and missionaries, and I will be purchasing many copies for many friends who will benefit from doing some "marriage maintenance" to protect their own God-given ministries.

Steve Jones
President, Missionary Church

Chapter 1
How it Began

I remember it like it was yesterday. I walked into our bedroom late at night. Our three young children had been asleep for hours. Sandi was already in bed, and she was quietly sobbing. As I walked to her side of the bed and sat down next to her this realization pressed down on me: "We are in trouble."

It was a strangely familiar feeling. In my early twenties I went sailing with my best friend, Greg, in Grand Traverse Bay in northern Michigan. We rented a catamaran and had skimmed several miles into the bay on strong winds when Greg asked if I wanted to try my hand sailing the boat. With rope in hand and leaning backwards over the cool, racing water, I caught too much wind in the sail and we capsized.

"Don't panic," Greg calmly urged, noticing the look of, well, panic on my face. "I know how to do this."

And sure enough, in a few minutes we righted the boat and continued sailing. Just as I began to relax we capsized again. But this time we didn't catch too much wind. The boat just seemed to topple over on its own.

So, we righted it a second time, and almost immediately we were back in the bay, clinging to the boat. "I think one of our hulls has a leak and is filling with water," Greg surmised. It was the only explanation.

So, there we were, a few miles off shore with no means of communication and no other boats in sight bobbing in that deep water. We were powerless to save ourselves. We were alone. We were in trouble.

Such was the fear that rose in my chest as I looked at Sandi's strained and despairing face in the dim light of our bedroom. We were in trouble, and for the first time in our thirteen years of marriage I was afraid.

Sitting next to her, defeated, exhausted and feeling certain that I was losing her, I said the only thing I knew to say, "We need help."

"We need help." Those three little words unlocked a door. I took the first and most crucial step – I named our reality. We were miles away from shore clinging to a leaking, capsized sailboat with no help in sight. And we both knew it, and I finally said it...

What is the reality of your marriage today? Do you know? Have you said it out loud yet?

This is a book written for those who want a good marriage AND a meaningful ministry. This is a book for couples who have veered off course, but want to get back on track. This is a book for leaders who lead themselves first, and then invite others into their journey.

What is the Promised Land for a marriage on mission?

- Intimacy – we know fully and are known fully

- Integration – we experience oneness without losing ourselves in the process
- Influence – we grow into leaders worth following; we have lives and relationships worth imitating as we imitate Christ
- Impact – we engage the mission of Jesus by making disciples who make disciples

This is our destination. We will become worthy citizens along the way through repentance, trust, and obedience. If you ask me, it's worth whatever effort or sacrifice required.

Hopefully as you hear our story, you will agree.

But first, it will help to understand how our marriage got into trouble.

Sandi and I were married in 1989, and our story read like something out of a Christian fairy tale. High school sweethearts, leaders in our youth ministry, role models to the younger students at church, athletic, good looking (especially Sandi), recent college graduates – we truly were living out our dreams. In our first year of marriage I served an internship in youth ministry and then accepted a call to serve as a youth pastor. Sandi and I made quite the team. We poured ourselves into those students and God just seemed to bless everything we touched. The youth ministry grew, I completed seminary, and we started a family.

I'm not proud to admit it, but I remember hearing about Christian couples who were struggling in their marriage, some divorcing. I recall how absolutely dumbfounded I was when yet another sad story emerged. "It isn't that hard," I said to myself. "If they would just trust God and follow what the Bible says they can have a great marriage, a strong marriage, a marriage just like ours." Little did I know...

In 1998 we served as short-term missionaries in Costa Rica and then moved to a new community as church planters. By the time we unpacked our boxes that fall we were in the early stages of planting a church in a city where we didn't know a single soul. We had two daughters (Megan, 3 and Emily, 1) and had just discovered we were pregnant! (Grant turned out to be our favorite souvenir from Costa Rica, but he was a full year ahead of schedule.)

On Easter Sunday in 1999 we launched the new church, and one month later Grant was born. To say we were overwhelmed and ill-prepared for the challenges and complexities we encountered that first year would be an understatement. I was so stressed out by the time Sandi was six months pregnant that I simply could not discuss possible baby names. Honestly, I just couldn't do it. Sandi insisted that we had to talk about a name for the boy – but I kept putting it off until the last possible moment. To choose a name meant that having our third child within a month of launching our first church was, in fact, a reality. It was too much.

But, ready or not, on May 17 Grant Thomas Blaylock made his grand entrance. While we were in the hospital for a couple of days with our newborn, we passed the hours watching home videos from the last year. As I sat with Sandi watching those videos I experienced a sobering and unsettling revelation. We were watching footage of our daughter Emily. I was either in the video with her, or behind the camera. I saw myself on the screen, I heard my voice coming through the speakers, but I could not remember being there.

For any of it...

There was a faint sense of the reality of what I was watching, but it had the quality of a distant memory with blurred edges. And then it hit me; I just missed out on the last year of my children's lives! So much had changed for the girls since we moved back from Costa Rica, and I hadn't been present enough to really experience it. And now it was gone, never to be reclaimed.

We brought Grant home the following day, and I stood by Emily's crib that night just looking at how big she was, how precious she was lying there asleep. For the first time in my life I knew that I had sacrificed too much – I had sacrificed something God never intended me to lay on the altar.

I wish I could say that night was my wake up call. I wish I could say that I picked up our baby girl and vowed to never again pursue ministry success as a higher priority than my family. Instead, I acknowledged my grief and went back to work the next day. This church wasn't going to plant itself and failure was not an option.

Fast-forward eighteen months. I am sitting in a restaurant with another pastor having breakfast. Everything seems fine. But at some point during our meeting I keep noticing that the walls seem to be moving toward me. The room feels like it is getting smaller and smaller. Soon I begin obsessing about getting out, it is all I can think about. I watch my friend's lips move as he talks to me. I hear my own voice answer. But the terror growing inside me as those walls begin crushing in drowns out everything else. My pulse begins racing. I honestly think I am having a heart attack or losing my mind. To this day it is one of the most terrifying experiences of my life.

Later that week, still not feeling well, I called my doctor. After a physical exam he began asking questions about my stress level. I was surprised. In fact, I was perturbed. What does my stress level have to do with it? Something is seriously wrong with me and it was his job to tell me what it was, prescribe a pill for it, and send me on my way. Instead he asked me to talk with a counselor. I agreed, but every fiber in my being stiffened at the thought.

"I am a pastor!" I chided myself. "Why should I need to talk with a counselor? What is he going to tell me that I don't already know?"

But, because of the incredible respect I had for our doctor, and with vivid images of the breakfast episode still fresh in my mind, I scheduled the appointment. My counselor's name was John, and during our first phone call I relayed to him some of the details of the incredible shrinking restaurant. He asked a few questions, and then said, "Tom, those are all the classic symptoms of a panic attack."

Stunned silence.

Over the next six months I met every week with John. We talked about my breathing. Yes, he gave me homework on how to breathe. Really? I actually needed to relearn how to breathe? (Those exercises proved very helpful, truth be told.)

We also talked about the pressure I felt in my chest, and the heart palpitations. Again, the results of prolonged stress. I wasn't going to die, but some days I might wish for it!

The recurring theme during those weeks was my desire to resign as the pastor of the church we had just planted. Week after week I told John I didn't want to do this anymore, that I couldn't do this anymore. And week after week John told me I didn't have to – that there were many other worthwhile things I could do that would still honor God.

It was the guilt that I couldn't overcome. You don't have a baby and then abandon her because parenting is too hard. You suck it up and do what you have to do. Right?

So, I pressed on. My symptoms worsened. I quit answering the phone. I began avoiding people whenever possible, including my own family. If I heard someone walking toward my office my stomach tightened as I prepared for the possibility that they may need something from me. I felt absolutely spent – like I had nothing more to give.

Finally, lying in bed one night unable to sleep, Sandi turned toward me and said, "I think you need to resign." For her this was an extremely painful death of a dream, a concession she desperately wanted to avoid. For me it was a piece of wreckage to cling to as I floated helplessly in that deep water.

Two months later I resigned from the church. It was very messy. No one understood. People were hurt, disappointed, disillusioned. The guilt piled higher and higher, the sense of failure deepened. Soon that guilt and failure soured inside of me and began turning into anger. I was angry with Sandi for expecting something from me that I couldn't live up to. I was angry with our church members who told me I was doing the wrong thing, that I needed to stay. I was angry with myself for being so weak. But mostly, I was angry with God. I believed that God and I had made a deal, and he wasn't holding up his end of the bargain. Why would he lead us to plant this church and then abandon us when we needed him most?

I never wanted to be in vocational ministry again. Not only did I want out of ministry, I wanted out of church altogether. I became cynical, critical, judgmental, and downright mean. Sandi and I began arguing. There were many fights, many tears, and some harsh words that left scars. Some of those scars are still fading.

We went to marriage counseling. But after a few sessions I told Sandi we weren't going back. I wasn't willing or able to deal with my own issues. I just wanted to blame the broken church system for my ministry failures and Sandi for our marriage struggles. We were both in a lot of pain, but trying desperately to hold it together for the kids. We also felt incredibly embarrassed. How could we fall so far so fast?

Then the night came when Sandi quit fighting. I could see the look of resignation in her eyes. As the tears trickled down she just got up, and without a word went to bed. She had given up. For a long time I sat alone in our living room. I knew that I was losing her; I knew that we were losing us. I knew that we needed help.

As I gently opened the door to our bedroom and walked over to her I was ready to fight. The difference? I was ready to begin fighting for our marriage.

From Sandi

As I reflect on the past several years and how God has worked in my marriage and ministry, I am both humbled and hopeful. I'm humbled because writing this book exposes some embarrassing things about my life. I am humbled to think that somehow God will use my story to help others. But I am hopeful because I believe as I obey God and share my story God will continue to bring healing into my life and to others as a result. I pray for you and trust that God has already started a work to bring hope. My prayer is that you will have the courage to obey and take the steps of faith that God is calling you to.

Chapter 2
Fighting for Your Marriage

*My husband and I have never considered divorce. Murder
sometimes, but never divorce.* ~ Joyce Brothers

"A happy marriage is the union of two good forgivers."
~ Ruth Bell Graham

The worst fight Sandi and I had during those long days
following my burn out as a church planter came late one night
after watching the movie *Fight Club*.

The movie (although not in my top 10) connected with some of
the angst I was feeling. It is a dark comedy about psychological
breakdown, the impact of consumerism on culture, and what it
means to be a real man. What is the essence of manhood and
self-respect in *Fight Club*? Fighting. At first they fight other
men, but ultimately they fight against the broken system that
enslaves them and attempts to define their identity and worth.

Suffice it to say that I really liked the movie and Sandi really,
really hated it. In the argument that ensued a dam broke loose.
I had never seen her so angry, so hurt. I had never felt so
frustrated or so cynical. It got ugly, and I said some things that
I deeply regret to this day.

She started packing. She was going to leave and stay with her
mother (who lived over an hour away). She simply said, "I
can't stay here with you tonight."

Click.

"She is leaving me. This is really happening..."

Let's just say I had a moment of clarity as she turned away and began walking from the room. Here is what I knew for certain in that instant:

- I love my wife.

- I don't want her to leave.

- I keep hurting her, and I don't know how to stop.

- I need help.

OK men, let's be honest. The first two realizations are obvious. We love our wives and we don't want them to leave. Fair enough, it's a starting point. But what about the next two?

I had become critical toward Sandi. I was defensive about the simplest things. Guilt and anger welled up inside of me and kept spilling over. She didn't deserve it, but I didn't know how to stop it.

"I need help." This was the turning point for me, and eventually for us.

"*We* are in trouble and *I* need help."

Until that night I had been waiting for Sandi to change. Until that night I believed the majority of my problems were the result of a broken church system that used and discarded pastors. Until that night I was beyond help. Why? Because I refused to take ownership for my own stuff, my own sin, my unique contribution. God's goodness leads to repentance, and repentance leads to life.

What made the difference? Sandi communicated to me in no uncertain terms that if I continued treating her poorly and speaking to her with disrespect and anger she would remove herself from my company (at least for one night). She made no attempt to control my bad behavior, instead she reminded me that she had the power to stay or to leave, and she was ready to use it. She established a boundary.

It was a slap in the face. One that I desperately needed.

Here were the initial steps we took to mend our marriage. (Please don't think of these steps as a "just add water" program to fix your marriage, they would have meant nothing without her healthy boundaries and my heart change.)

1. Finding a safe place for a dangerous conversation

2. Respecting the process...and the processing

3. Choosing to love and waiting on the feelings

Finding a safe place for a dangerous conversation

First, I reached out to our pastor and asked for help. Since he was a friend it was tricky, but I was pretty desperate and decided to risk the potential loss of respect.

We were blessed to have a pastor who was also a gifted counselor. He exuded warmth – we never feared judgment with him. And, when you are struggling in your marriage and are supposed to be Christian leaders, this is the kind of person you want! As we met with him and began talking honestly about the way we felt about each other, our marriage, and our struggles, things began breaking loose. We didn't resolve anything during those first few months, but the important issues emerged and the right conversations began.

Looking back I think the role of Christian counseling was essential for us. Without those very raw discussions under the watchful and experienced eye of someone who knew and cared about us we would have continued our downward spiral. But here's the thing, he never gave us the magic formula for marital bliss. He never said, "OK, here's what you need to do." He asked good questions, he gave us honest feedback, he listened intently, and he made a few really good suggestions. He also prayed for us and with us. Our relationship struggles became part and parcel of a bigger and deeper relationship. To love and trust God meant loving and trusting one another, even if we might get hurt in the process.

I am fascinated by how communication dynamics shift when a skilled counselor is injected. I have studied this phenomenon for the past fifteen years in my role as leadership coach. Honestly, it's pretty incredible.

But why? This is what my experience would suggest:

The presence of an objective and loving third party helps move us past either/or, all-or-nothing confrontations toward a bigger (and better) picture. Many times I am right, AND she is right. Often I am wrong, AND she is wrong. (And yes, several times she was right and I was wrong – but who's counting?) A good counselor can step back and describe to us the underlying patterns he sees and restate what our spouse is saying in a way that gets through our defenses. They help us see aspects of our situation in a new light, and often this stirs hope and humility (and without hope and humility we don't stand a chance).

Good counselors expose blind spots. One of my greatest difficulties in communicating with Sandi was that I didn't know what I didn't know. In other words, I had gaps in my self-awareness that were sabotaging my best attempts. And the funny thing about those blind spots, you can't see them!

One of my blind spots was an extreme sensitivity to complaining. Anytime Sandi would express dissatisfaction with anything (her job, the kids, our house – it didn't matter) I took it personally. It was like she was saying, "You are a failure because my job is stressful and I'm not getting along with my boss!" All she was trying to do as a verbal processor was ventilate and talk about her day, but I reacted to these complaints as personal attacks. This was a significant issue that plagued us for years, and we will discuss it at greater length in the next chapter.

Good counselors are always good listeners. How many people in your life listen closely to every word you say? They are rare finds in our world of constant noise and endless self-expression. There were things that Sandi and I had been trying to get off our chests for months, but who would listen? We certainly weren't doing a spectacular job of listening to one another. We didn't want to air our dirty laundry in front of our friends. And, thankfully, we didn't want to speak ill of one another (we avoided speaking to people about each other with contempt – contempt usually comes just before lawyers get involved).

So, when Sandi was finally able to express herself (without fearing my defensiveness) it was healing. Sometimes you just need to know you've been heard. Sometimes you need a little reassurance that you aren't crazy! And, sometimes you need to hear your own voice and listen to yourself talk without interruption. It can be very eye opening, sometimes revolutionary.

Where is a safe place for a dangerous conversation about your marriage? Any place the two of you can sit down with a qualified Christian counselor and talk openly about your relationship. The research backs this up,[1] so think long and hard about starting your journey to a mended marriage with the help of a good counselor.

Respect the process...and the processing

There was a resignation in her voice that alarmed me last night—in some ways it has been like watching a woman making preparations for her life after the divorce is final. I know that sounds dramatic, but I think this is the level of drama that Sandi is feeling internally right now... I am supposed to be the one who makes her happy. But I have failed. And after 18 years I have come to the place where I have lost hope that Sandi will ever

---

[1] Worthington, Everett L. Jr. (Editor) and Eric L. Johnson (Editor), Joshua N. Hook (Editor), and Jamie D. Aten (Editor), *Evidence-Based Practices for Christian Counseling and Psychotherapy*, (Downers Grove, IL: Intervarsity Press, 2013).

truly be happy or content. **I have come to the place where I am now looking beyond our marriage to feel like I am successful at something important.**

~ *Tom's journal, August 1, 2007*

Sandi was preparing herself for life on her own (whether still married to me or not), and I was starting to look elsewhere for something to make me feel successful. Like I said, we were in trouble.

The most frustrating aspect of the downward spiral was our inability to communicate without arguing. For a few years we just avoided topics like church, God, ministry, my work, my burn out, and her transition from stay-at-home pastor's wife into full time technology sales. In other words, we could only talk about the shallow stuff, the safe stuff.

Like many struggling couples we retreated to a child-centered marriage. Everything we talked about revolved around our three kids. Their schooling, their sports, their schedules, their friends, and their youth group activities became the topics that dominated most conversations.

"If we can't be happily married, at least we can be good parents," was the thinking.

If nothing else, this did give us something constructive to focus on. So, we poured into the kids. They were all involved in multiple sport teams, the girls took music lessons, Grant joined a trap shooting team, and I volunteered as the youth leader at church and started pouring into more kids. We were very busy, but we were slowly sinking.

Seeking out Christian counseling got the ball rolling for us. The next barrier was figuring out how to talk to each other, how to listen to each other, and how to get a better handle on our issues.

God helped us when we needed it most. Here were the two handles he gave to get us unstuck:

1. Understanding the dynamics for internal processors and external processors

2. Writing to one another, and then talking

The first "aha" moment for me was when I finally understood what it meant that Sandi was an extroverted, external processor and I was a slightly introverted, internal processor. Why is this such a big deal? Let's define our terms first and then connect the dots:

Internal Processors

- Don't like to speak until they have thought through the issue completely

- Require time and silence to process

- Sometimes are too committed to their conclusions prior to collaboration

External Processors

- Say whatever they are thinking (and may not agree with everything they say)

- Literally process externally – they think out loud

- Sometimes lack the discretion and discipline called for by the situation

What were my needs as an internal processor? I needed time and solitude to process how I felt and what I wanted to communicate. If Sandi pushed me, in the heat of the moment to respond, I would feel overwhelmed and frustrated. I would then use my anger to shut down a conversation I was not ready to engage in.

Sandi would interpret this reticence as an attempt to hide something, or worse, a passive aggressive ploy designed to hurt or frustrate her. (And, to be honest, sometimes that's exactly what it was.)

Internal processors hate to be interrupted when sharing their thoughts. We spend a great deal of time and energy thinking through exactly what we want to say – choosing each word with precision. Until we can communicate all of it we are not ready to defend or explain certain points along the way.

Sandi wanted to play verbal tennis, and bat the ball back and forth across the net in a free flowing exchange. I wanted to write a meticulous letter, deliver it to her, let her read it, and then listen to her response.

Sandi's need as an external processor was that she needed me to listen to whatever she had to say without judgment. She needed me to hear her out, give her the grace to change her mind along the way if necessary, and only after we talked at length begin formulating any plan of action. Most of all, she needed me to be secure enough not to react defensively as she processed. If required to verbally filter too much in the early stages of the conversation, she would shut down.

I would continually sabotage Sandi's attempts by requiring too much precision too early and by reacting personally to comments that were not intended critically. I wanted her to communicate with me the same way I wanted to communicate with her. It's OK to want that, but if we make those kinds of demands a hill to die on we are on a suicide mission.

As Sandi's frustration grew she would "up the ante" by expressing her feelings in stronger and louder language. She was trying to get my attention, hoping for my open engagement. But this always had the opposite effect. I would dismiss these larger than life exertions by slipping into parent-child thinking. I am not proud to admit it, but I would often view myself as the parent and Sandi as the child who was having a tantrum, but who would calm down eventually. (No wonder she was so frustrated...)

Once we began learning about our personality differences and how these dynamics were impacting our communication (a huge win for us) we were able to find a new way. We decided to honor both my needs as an internal processor and her needs as an external processor. Here's how we did it:

1. I would start by journaling.

2. I would then email Sandi excerpts from my journal.

3. She would read these emails, and respond to me in writing.

4. Then we would discuss those issues, the dangerous ones with a counselor, and the safer ones on our own.

That's it. This simple practice brought about an incredible breakthrough! We were able to talk about things that had been taboo for years, with very little anger. I felt like I was being heard without interruption or pressure to say too much too soon. Sandi was able to respond to the emails and then verbally process with me at a later time. She also had a couple friends to process with as needed.

For this to work we each had to give something up. I had to allow Sandi to process, especially her negative feelings, without getting defensive and shutting her down (or trying to fix anything). Sandi had to exercise patience and discipline – giving me the time to talk when I was ready and allowing written communication to serve as an onramp to constructive dialogue.

We continue writing to one another to this day; it has been an extremely effective practice these past eight years. For us, it has become healthy arguing with training wheels. There may come a day when we won't need to do this, but I am in no hurry to go back to the old ways. This practice has taught us mutual submission and has given us a practical way to honor and celebrate one another's differences.

Choosing to love and waiting on the feelings

Even with these breakthrough experiences, pressing issues remained: How do you show love to someone you may not like on a particular day? How do you serve someone who makes you angry? How do you open yourself up to someone you feel is untrustworthy?

Simple answer: You make a choice to love, and then you follow through.

Simple, but very hard.

As our marriage started getting stronger we kept getting sidetracked. Something would happen, or something would be said that dredged up bad feelings. The smallest thing could tip that first domino and another evening went down the toilet.

We learned to begin intentionally loving each other and we trusted that the good feelings would come in time. And, like so many things in life, it is often the smallest things that make the biggest difference.

Here are a few ideas that worked for us. We hope one of them sparks a good idea that works for you!

1. *Learn to speak your spouse's love language*

In his book, *The 5 Love Languages*, author and pastor Gary Chapman describes the primary ways each of us receives love. The five options are:

- Words of affirmation
- Acts of service
- Receiving gifts
- Quality time

- Physical touch

We read this book years before, but were failing miserably in applying it. Sandi's primary love language is quality time, mine is acts of service. So, how did we show love to one another? Sandi tried spending a lot of time with me, and I began working on projects around the house.

Fail.

The more she pressed to be with me, the more I wanted to work on that deck or build that retaining wall! Until that fateful Saturday morning – I slept in late, and by the time I made my way into the kitchen Sandi was already gone. Since I usually can't find the bread without her help, I started looking for her. She wasn't in the house. Then, I looked out our window and saw one of the most beautiful sights ever to visit God's green earth; Sandi was in the driveway washing and waxing my pickup truck.

I got so excited! The first thing I did was grab our camera and run outside to take a picture. (My friends would never believe it otherwise!) Then I just sat there for several minutes watching her. (Who needs breakfast?) Those images are burned into my mind. No, they are burned onto my heart. Why? Because that's what love looks like to me.

Following Sandi's example, I began going out of my way to spend more time with her. For instance, if I was watching TV in the living room and she walked in and wanted to talk, I actually turned off the TV, turned to face her, and listened to what she had to say. Then I got really crazy and started planning date nights – I even went so far as to arrange childcare! I know, radical.

2. Try a new recipe for romance

Romantic feelings dry up during periods of conflict and struggle. Passion fades when you don't feel safe and appreciated. What can you do to turn up the heat?

First, a disclaimer: Before we talk about practical steps to spark romance in your marriage, we need to talk about one of God's commands for married couples. In 1 Corinthians 7:5 Paul writes:

Do not deprive each other except perhaps by mutual consent and for a time, so that you may devote yourselves to prayer. Then come together again so that Satan will not tempt you because of your lack of self-control.

Translation? Do not withhold sex. Do not use sex as a weapon. Do not treat sex as a lever to get what you want.

Our ongoing commitment (let's be honest, Sandi's ongoing commitment) to this Biblical principle saved our marriage. A healthy and consistent sexual relationship pours glue onto a marriage, and in the long run that glue can hold things together when the going gets rough. This does not give husbands the right to demand sex from their wives, but a wise wife will fight for her marriage by pursuing physical intimacy even during the hard times.

OK, back to the romance! We found ourselves low on creative ideas for bringing back some laughter and sizzle into our relationship. So, Sandi brought a book home one night called, *101 Nights of Grrreat Romance* by Lara Corn. At first I thought it was silly – like we actually needed to read a book on how to be romantic! I resisted. But then I thought about how far we had already come, and decided to give it a try.

I was not disappointed.

One of the cool things about this book was the sealed envelopes for the husband or wife. Inside these envelopes were specific instructions on how to plan a date that would make a memory and bring some fun and passion back.

- One night I rented a tandem bicycle in downtown Lansing and we pedaled up and down the Grand River before going out for a nice meal.

- One night Sandi set up a tent in our back woods and led me on a wild goose chase that circled back to our own property. Let's just say we could have roasted marshmallows that night without a campfire...

Soon we began improvising and coming up with our own crazy and wonderful plans. Whoever was planning the date asked this question; "What would the other person enjoy and how can I make them feel loved?" Sandi took me to a gun range. I surprised her by inviting all of our friends to meet up for dinner on our anniversary. We planned a trip to Mackinac Island where we hiked, wandered the downtown shops, ate some great meals, and just spoiled each other for a couple of days. That particular trip will always stand out for me because Sandi went to so much trouble to plan certain things she knew

I would like. It was her intentionality that spoke love to me, and that love made me feel strong and hopeful.

3. Plan special trips

Getting away together every few months became a big part of our turn around. Sometimes they were simple, overnight trips to Lake Michigan. Occasionally they were bigger outings, like the Mackinac Island trip. And, on rare occasions, they were weeklong adventures to faraway places like the western Caribbean aboard a cruise ship.

Where you go or how much money you spend really isn't the point. The important thing is that you are going someplace you both enjoy, you are spending lots of time together in a relaxed environment, and you are making a tangible investment in your relationship. By taking these trips a few times a year you can begin building momentum and making the kind of memories that pull you together.

Here are a few reasons why you need to start planning that next trip:

They get you out of the house, away from the kids, and beyond the reach of the hundreds of stressors that rob your focus from one another. Sandi found it very difficult to relax at home with young children. Everywhere she looked she found reminders of more work to do. Dirty dishes in the sink, smudges on the window from a curious 5 year old, a dog that needed grooming, or the bills that still had to be sorted and paid.

You get the idea. In fact, 99% of you know exactly what I am talking about. So, since the "To Do List" is an eternal reality for most of us, don't fight it – choose to get away for a day or two. Yes, it's inconvenient and can be expensive, but every penny we invested on those trips has been worth it ten times over.

Another aspect that sometimes gets overlooked is planning trips together gives you something to talk about and look forward to. This may not sound like such a big deal, but when you are struggling to communicate about anything more significant than the next soccer practice it becomes a really big deal.

Planning our cruise, which excursions we might take, what we would wear to the formal dinner, even deciding upon which seasick medications to bring were all wins for us. They were wins because we were able to find agreement, we both made suggestions that built a sense of ownership, and the more we talked about it the more excited we became.

A word of caution for the guys: don't try to surprise your wife by pulling off that fairy tale ending, shock and awe trip. I made a few runs at this, and they usually backfired.

Here's why:

- There is no planning or dreaming together—she is not consulted and has to just go along with whatever he plans.

- She doesn't get a chance to talk about the trip beforehand. For many people the anticipation and conversation planning the trip is almost as important as the trip itself (this is certainly true for Sandi).

- She doesn't want to be awestruck once every three years, and then ignored the rest of the time. Let's be honest, sometimes husbands plan the big reveal and break the budget out of a sense of guilt. Better to bring her one rose a month than a dozen roses once a year...

Finally, special trips are love-language-rich environments. Think about it.

You are spending a lot of time together (quality time). You are having tons of conversation, and with the slightest effort each can find ways to express gratitude (words of affirmation). Making that special purchase before the trip, or even that spontaneous treasure picked up while shopping can turn into meaningful gifts (receiving gifts). She irons my shirt before dinner, or I find kindling to start the fire (acts of service). And maybe the best of all – no kids, no interruptions, no phones, and nowhere you need to be? Sounds like the perfect environment for some one-on-one interaction (physical touch). Yes, I am talking about sex, but don't limit this love language just to sex. Holding hands, napping together, shoulder rubs, and just sitting close together while watching a movie – especially when not equated with foreplay – say, "I love you just because."

From Sandi

"I choose us" is a line from one of my favorite movies, *The Family Man.* In this movie, the main character, played by Nicholas Cage, is struggling to choose between career success or family commitment. When given the decision to move back into the city or stay in their small town, his wife says, "I choose us". She sacrifices her own goals to serve him and make him a priority. She is basically saying that she will do whatever it takes to prioritize their relationship. I have said, "I choose us" many times throughout my married life. John 15:13 says, *"Greater love has no one than this, that he lay down his life for his friends."* I believe marriage calls for that level of love and commitment. I have to lay down the "me" for the "us".

I choose us.

I remember the argument after the *Fight Club* movie well. It was an emotional time and I felt alone and abandoned. My fairy tale dream of happily ever after died that night and I was terrified. I put Tom in a corner – he couldn't make me happy no matter how hard he tried, so he was feeling defensive and blaming me. I looked to Tom to meet needs that only God could meet and I became overly dependent. I finally realized he was not the solution to my problems. It was as if blinders fell from my eyes and I saw clearly that this man could never make me happy, and that made me angry. I was furious at Tom for being controlling even though I was the one who gave him that control. I knew I needed to take a stand – for me and for him. Yes, he was treating me disrespectfully and like a child, but I had repeatedly allowed it to continue, unchallenged. We were both at fault and had developed some unhealthy patterns. I needed to trust God and take ownership of my own struggles instead of placing unrealistic expectations on my husband. I believe this was my first step toward healing. At the time I felt alone. "Is God good even if my husband doesn't protect and provide?" Can God come through when people let me down?

Here are the steps I began taking that night.

1. Acceptance. Tom is not meeting my needs. I accepted the reality that Tom could not and would not meet all of my needs. I had to repent of my own idolatry and release Tom from unrealistic expectations.

2. Protection. I will establish healthy boundaries. I will not allow Tom to treat me with disrespect or anger. I will say, "no" when appropriate.

3. Surrender. I give up trying to control Tom's behavior. I give up control and surrender my future into God's hands. To me this felt like the death of a dream.

4. Trust. I am looking to God to meet my needs. I am not alone but I feel alone. I will move forward in faith, pursuing God and all that he wants me to do.

I wish I could say that God gave instant healing and we

never struggled again. Instead, God gave us small glimpses of relational intimacy. We took baby steps and kept moving forward in hope and faith.

Counseling helped us and gave me an emotionally safe place to practice saying no. We made quite a commitment to finding a Christian counselor but it was well worth the money and effort. I didn't like the hard work of becoming an independent woman, but I loved the respect I gained from Tom. I found my voice!

Writing was another powerful method of communication for us during that dark time. At first, writing letters and emails felt like a sacrifice to me because I wanted to talk everything out instead of going through the long process of writing and waiting for a response. My external processing brain was challenged, but I knew that it was a step in the right direction. At least we were bringing up difficult subjects and making progress with them. If I could just be patient and allow Tom the time he needed to process in writing, then we could have a more beneficial and constructive conversation afterward. While it wasn't ideal, it was progress. I had to surrender my communication preferences and submit to a process that could work for both of us.

Journaling and writing to Tom spurred my growth as I practiced the disciplines of quiet and solitude. This still doesn't come naturally to me but I am acquiring a taste for it.

In a tangible way writing, instead of blurting every thought in my head, teaches discretion in communication. It is not always appropriate to say everything on my mind! (WHAT? Still hard for me to believe.) As Tom said, we still write to each other often. Just the other day I was feeling very discouraged but I couldn't quite figure out why. Tom was out of town for almost a week so we didn't get to talk much about it. In the old days, I would meet him at the door and tell him everything bothering me, fully expecting him to engage in deep conversation and process with me. He wouldn't even have time to unpack his bags and I would demand his full attention. This was the part of me that had to change. So in this recent situation, I waited a couple days and reflected on my struggle as he recovered from his trip. I went to God first and prayed for clarity. I wrote about it and tried to bottom line it as much as possible before I brought it up to Tom. So when I did bring it up, we were able to have a helpful conversation. This is an example of a healthy give and take. I served him by giving him space first, and he served me by engaging in conversation when I needed it.

During the difficult years, I made a commitment to respect Tom regardless of how I felt in the moment. As I studied the scriptures it was clear that I was to do this as an act of obedience to God. Contemporary culture is confused by Biblical love and respect in marriage. We seem to understand that love should be unconditional, but respect is earned. Ephesians chapter 5 tells me to respect my husband...period. I am not to wait for Tom to do something worthy of respect before I obey this command. Respecting

Tom helps him love me, and Tom's love for me helps me to respect him, but someone has to go first. I think Tom was always trying to do a good job of loving me, but I wasn't always trying to do a good job of respecting him. I needed to focus on respect.

One thing I did to honor this commitment was speaking respectfully to Tom both privately and publicly. (I allowed myself to vent sometimes to a couple trusted friends to keep me sane and accountable.) Nothing positive came when I put Tom down or complained in public. I also chose to speak Tom's love languages of acts of service and physical touch.

Loving actions precede loving feelings.

I made choices to do things around the house that he would appreciate – like washing his truck. I tried to keep the countertops clear. I worked with him in the garden. I looked for things to do with and for Tom to show that I loved him. I did simple things knowing that he would see them as acts of love. As Tom saw me investing in the relationship in a way that was meaningful to him, he became more willing to invest in the relationship in ways that were meaningful to me. As I moved closer to him, he moved closer to me. I was willing to go first.

I intentionally cultivated physical intimacy with Tom as a spiritual act of worship. I understood that he loved God and was working hard to serve Him wholeheartedly. He needed to see that I believed in him and was holding onto the hope of a future together. I went so far as planning times for physical intimacy whenever God brought it to my mind. I would text or call Tom during the day to tell him I was thinking of him at that moment and tonight would be a good night for romance. Sometimes by the time evening came I was no longer thinking positively about it, but I had made a commitment and would follow through. I believe this simple commitment empowered Tom to step up to the changes God was calling him to make. I willingly offered myself and trusted that God would provide for my needs while I loved Tom in a tangible way. This simple and consistent commitment spoke volumes of love and loyalty to Tom and gave him strength and security.

As part of this commitment to speak Tom's love languages of physical touch and acts of service, I planned a trip to Mackinac Island. I remember putting lots of work into writing multiple "Top 10 Lists."

- Top 10 things I love about Tom

- Top 10 memories as a family

- Top 10 vacation memories

- Top 10 favorite memories of dating

- Top 10 romantic memories

I pulled out a new top 10 list and presented it to Tom at each meal during the trip. I printed the lists on paper, rolled them like a scroll, and tied them with red ribbon. I filled him with positive things about our marriage and it helped to bring renewed hope for a better future. Writing those top 10 lists ahead of time also reminded me of all the good times. It helped me focus on what was good in our relationship and it was a beautiful thing.

Chapter 3
Reversing Marital Meltdown

What you want
(Ooh) Baby, I got
(Ooh) What you need
(Ooh) Do you know I've got it
(Ooh) All I'm askin'
(Ooh) Is for a little respect when you come home
(just a little bit)
Hey baby (just a little bit) when you get home

~ Aretha Franklin's "Respect"

Sandi and I began doing some of the right things, and our marriage started to mend. We were scheduling get-aways, learning to speak one another's love language, rekindling romance, and meeting with a Christian counselor. Those behaviors had their desired effect – we were moving toward one another again and starting to talk about what God may have for us in the future.

And then, we hit a snag. A deeper issue emerged, and it was a big one...

A true partnership was not possible for us, after all. There was a missing ingredient that stopped us in our tracks: deep down, I didn't respect Sandi. And she knew it...

She wrote.

I believe that Tom views my personality type as weak and needy. Even if I shine who God created me to be, it will not be enough to earn Tom's respect. He will view me as being a beautiful person full of life and love, but not a peer to be taken seriously.

~ Email excerpt, August 27, 2007

I will never forget reading those words. I knew she was right – I had lost respect for her. Slowly I began taking on more and more of a parenting role in our relationship. Honestly, we probably were leaning in this direction from our wedding day, but it didn't really cause problems the first 10 years. Well, the time had come to pay (with interest).

Sandi believed that no matter how hard she tried; it would never be enough to earn my respect. At the end of the day, she knew I didn't see her as a peer – as a real partner.

There was no point denying it. In fact, this is what I wrote in my journal a few weeks earlier:

One thing that does stand out to me is this - my level of respect for Sandi has slowly eroded over the years. My love for her is strong. My commitment to her is strong. But do I view her as a peer? Do I trust her to advise me on important decisions? No.

~ Tom's journal, August 1, 2007

Bottom line, there must be at least three components in any healthy marriage:

1. Mutual love

2. Mutual trust

3. Mutual respect

We had the first two, but it wasn't enough. In fact, the lack of respect was undermining our trust (it was undermining everything, really). Unless we could learn to navigate these white waters and find a way to change course, our vision of an integrated marriage and ministry was just a pipe dream. If I didn't view Sandi as a full partner and take her input seriously we didn't stand a chance.

Here are the steps we took to reverse course. And, it all started with Sandi.

1. The power of "no"

In the last chapter I told the story of our worst fight ever. The turning point that night was a decision Sandi made to say a very simple word.

"No."

"No, I will not stay here with you tonight if you keep speaking to me that way."

Without trying to control my behavior she calmly informed me of her intention to stay with her mom if I continued expressing anger and disrespect. By establishing this boundary she stood up to me and called me out. If I wanted her to stay I would have to respect her words. If I didn't want to be alone, I would have to take her seriously.

Sandi had found her voice, and I respected her for it. She was willing to step away from me and stand on her own two feet if necessary. I had been seeing her for so long through the "parent-child" lens that this assertion of power to determine her own course initially stunned me.

I didn't know what to do with it. I couldn't argue against it. I couldn't ignore it. The only choice I had was to respect it and begin to own some of my shortcomings.

Sandi was, in fact, recognizing and honoring a personal boundary.

In their book, *Boundaries*, Dr. Henry Cloud and Dr. John Townsend write:

"Boundaries define us. They define what *is me* and what is *not me*. A boundary shows me where I end and someone else begins, leading me to a sense of ownership" (p. 29).

They go on to say; "We are responsible *to* others, and *for* ourselves," (p. 30).

Instead of trying to control me, Sandi was taking responsibility for herself. She would no longer allow herself to be treated as if she were the cause of my unhappiness. If I persisted, she would walk out of the room. In that simple "no" she communicated that she would be responsible to me, but no longer for me. I would now have to take ownership for my own problems; they were on my side of the property line.

In that one act of loving defiance a chain reaction ignited that restored a sense of hope and dignity to our relationship. The parent-child facade fractured that night, and two responsible adults faced one another, and their issues.

2. A difficult choice

There is an old saying; "Be careful what you wish for." It's one of those sayings you don't appreciate when you're young, but the cool irony is not lost on you later in life.

I wished for a partner I could respect and depend upon. I wished for a spouse with internal strength and fortitude. I wished for a wife who could stand on her own two feet and join me as a peer in discerning and living out God's calling on our lives.

And, in the coming months, that's exactly what began to happen.

The problem? I didn't like it.

In fact, some days, I hated it. Why? Simply put, I liked being in charge. I liked making the big decisions and just informing Sandi about them. I didn't like her questioning me about everything. I didn't like the way she reserved the right to her "no", even when I was convinced otherwise.

It was a lot of work. Decisions that could have been made in three minutes now dragged out for days! Sandi asked me questions I wasn't prepared to answer. She had such a different way of looking at things! I felt off-balance. Honestly, this wasn't what I bargained for.

There were times I resorted to my old ways, and tried to shut her down with anger. If she didn't cower I resorted to other tactics. I can be very strong willed, and if I felt she pushed back too hard I would shut her out and go silent for days on end. Power struggles ensued, and Sandi's fortitude was tested. Would she hold her ground or cave?

Thankfully, for the most part, she held her ground. She displayed a great deal of strength and grace during my detox period, which lasted over a year. Eventually I had a choice to make; do I want to be in charge or do a want a partnership with my wife?

I chose partnership. I began learning the ways of a servant leader. I developed an appetite for mutual submission. I started growing into a leader who understood the power of covenant. And this kingdom principle emerged: *covenant faithfulness precedes kingdom fruitfulness.*

3. Unpacking very old bags

I mentioned in the last chapter an extreme sensitivity I had to any complaining from Sandi. Here is how it usually worked:

Sandi would express dissatisfaction with something. An example was her dislike for our mucky backyard. Our Michigan property backed up to a river, and most of our yard was a swampy mess when we first bought the house.

Step 1: Sandi is unhappy about something. Check.

As a good husband, it's my job to make her happy, right? So, logically speaking, if I can fix the problem she will be happy.

Step 2: Devise plan to fix the problem. Check.

In this case the problem was significant. Our soil held a lot of water, and our yard was low. Two choices emerged: dig a pond or install drain tile.

Step 3: Implement the plan and fix the problem. Check.

I went with option two, and $2,000 and many backbreaking hours later we had drain tile installed.

Step 4: Problem solved, wife is now happy! (Crickets...)

This is where we ran into difficulty. Sandi was still not totally satisfied. For one thing, we couldn't really afford the $2,000. I just wrote the check and hoped for the best! Second, there were still areas in our backyard that were wet. In fact, the following year we had to install a catch basin (Cha-Ching!). But most of all, Sandi was not happy with how she was treated through the process. She was barely consulted. I went into problem solving mode and just made it happen. She felt no ownership of the solution I devised because she was never asked. This spurred resentment, and the resentment came out in more complaining about the wet yard.

Step 5: I did my best to fix the problem. No more complaining!

Now things were getting dicey. I did not want to hear anything more about that stupid backyard! She is angry because I never really listened to her. I am angry because my best efforts weren't good enough. Any complaint now sounded like this to me; "You aren't good enough. You will never be good enough. No matter how hard you try you are going to fail."

Step 6: Shut her down with anger or silence.

Sandi's complaints hit a raw nerve. It was so painful for me that, at one point, our counselor advised her to only share complaints with me one day a week, at a set time. (That did wonders for our communication!) When the pain got too intense I reacted. First, I would attempt to literally shut her up through anger. "You see how hard I tried! Why are you so ungrateful?" If that didn't work, I would withdraw and go silent. For Sandi, this constituted psychological torture. She feared abandonment, and I knew how to push that button...

Step 7: Silence, distance, and both of us feeling hurt and lonely. Check.

This is the sad state we found ourselves in way too often. We began creating an unspoken list of forbidden topics, and that list kept getting longer. Our communication grew more shallow. We played it safe. Like two fighters in the ring too tired to keep swinging, we retreated to our respective corners. The general feeling was, "If we keep our distance, at least we won't keep hurting each other."

What was the trigger for all of this? What baggage had I brought into our marriage that set us up for all of this grief?

Here is a big clue from my journal:

I have developed a hyper-sensitivity to any complaints by Sandi. If Sandi says she would like a four-bedroom house I feel like a failure for only providing her with a three-bedroom house. If Sandi says she wants a bigger camper, nicer vacations, or new kitchen cabinets I feel like a failure. At first I feel guilty and then I get angry. Deep down I want to be the hero that makes all of her dreams come true, but as I listen to her mourn her unfulfilled dreams (or even make a passing comment about how nice it would be to drive a newer vehicle) I am reminded over and over again that I am not a hero.

I have come to the place where I have lost hope that Sandi will ever be a content person. And this loss of hope has significantly impacted my energy level in this relationship - I feel like no matter what I do it will never be enough, so I really don't have the motivation to do too much - just enough to get by and keep the peace.

~ Tom 's journal, August 23, 2007

Did you catch that? I had significant boundary issues. I made myself responsible for something that belonged to Sandi – her own feelings of happiness and contentment. I saw it as my job to "make her happy" (whether she liked it or not!). So, if she was ever unhappy it was my fault. And that made me feel guilty. Which made me feel like a failure. Which made me angry.

These feelings of failure stretched back to my early childhood. As a boy of ten I believed it was my responsibility to rescue my mother from a bad marriage. My dad was an alcoholic, and they were both very unhappy. My dream was to be the hero who rescued mom, who brought her the happiness I felt she deserved but would never experience while married to dad.

If that was my job, then I failed. If mom's happiness was my responsibility, then I let her down.

No wonder I was so defensive toward Sandi. No wonder I am still retraining my mind to view myself as responsible **to** those I love, but not **for** them. My recovery from this type of co-dependency has been recently aided through my participation in Al-Anon. If someone you love has a problem with alcohol or another addictive substance, Al-Anon can be a great source of health and hope (for YOU, not the addict). I would encourage you to find out more at www.al-anon.org.

Jesus told us that we would know a tree by its fruit. The fruit on a tree tells you what kind of tree it is, whether apple or peach. And, ultimately, the fruit comes from the root. If the fruit is bad, the root is bad.

It is this beneath-the-soil work that is the hardest. Digging deep, examining the roots of our lives, our beliefs, and our responses is not for the faint of heart. On several occasions I gave up on the process. Ultimately, it took facing the probability of losing the one person on this planet I loved most to give me the courage and determination to press on.

Looking back, God gave us three stepping stones to cross the rapids:

1. Healthy boundaries (until Sandi said "no" I was unwilling to say "yes")

2. The choice of partnership over control (mutual submission)

3. Ownership and repentance of generational sin (unloading dysfunctional baggage)

Scientists tell us that 90% of an iceberg is under water. As the captain of the Titanic learned the hard way in 1912 (along with over 1,500 people who perished in the icy waters of the North Atlantic) it's what's below the waterline that will kill you.

Sandi and I were finally able to face and deal with the deep issues which plagued us for so long. We were ready to begin making progress. Filled with a sense of renewed hope and expectancy we started walking into what God had next for us – literally.

From Sandi

I do feel a bit funny communicating all these personal things on email, but it actually is working quite well. For some reason, just knowing that I have other people helping with this process makes me feel courage and strength to write down my thoughts. Usually I do not write down my reactions or my thoughts during a difficult time. I like to process verbally. But I appreciate that doing some of this hard communicating through writing is proving quite helpful. It allows me to review and see for myself some of my own areas of improvement and areas to celebrate growth. It also helps Tom because he can read the things that I write apart from the emotion and heat of the moment when I would usually be apt to share the struggles.

Sandi's journal entry, August 27, 2007

During this process I meditated on scripture often. Psalm 27:4 kept coming back to me, especially when I was feeling alone. I like the beautiful wording of the KJV, *"One thing I have desired of the Lord, that will I seek after; that I may dwell in the house of the Lord all the days of my life, to behold the beauty of the Lord and to inquire in his temple."* God was calling me to wholeheartedly desire, seek, and behold Him.

I needed to figure out a way to grow spiritually so I purchased a couple devotional books to help me focus my time alone with God. There are so many good ones! It really helps me to have a daily reading schedule to follow with some summary thoughts or statements to ponder. Tom doesn't usually use any devotional books so I had avoided them in the past. I made the decision to embrace a different method than Tom's. This was an essential step: I took ownership of my spiritual journey. This might sound like a small and obvious step, but for me it was a departure from a way of thinking that I had adopted from Tom. God created people with so many different personalities and ways to connect with him, why did I feel like the only way to practice spiritual disciplines was to mimic the exact ways that Tom did them?

I also rearranged my work schedule so that I could join a ladies' small group Bible study that became a lifeline for me in many ways. It connected me with godly women to process what I was learning out loud. This was NOT a husband gossip session and I would strongly recommend that you never complain about or belittle your spouse in any group setting – EVER. This small group allowed me to talk about spiritual formation and how I can best apply what I was learning to my daily life. I did have one friend that I talked to about my marriage struggles, but this person knew and respected Tom. It was a safe place to have difficult conversations as she challenged me to be a strong, godly wife while at the same time understanding the difficulty of my struggles. I stayed involved in our local church and focused on ministries that I could do without waiting for Tom to lead them.

I served God as an individual.

I was sometimes lonely and in need of connection. For a while I looked for connection in some unhealthy ways. I allowed my mind to wander and found myself drawn to an old friend, someone who used to care for me deeply and make me laugh. I innocently reconnected with him and was blown away by the intensity of my feelings. I was on the brink of an emotional affair and could have easily justified it in my mind. This temptation challenged my commitment to God and to Tom. Thankfully I shared my struggles with my trusted friend who helped with loving accountability. She helped me avoid a devastating loss and spoke truth and grace into my life. God wanted me to be faithful in my marriage, continue to work on my relationship with Him, and trust Him to meet my needs. Pursuing another relationship would have ruined everything and circumvented the steps I needed to take for growth. The easy way out isn't good for anyone!

Trust God and be faithful. I had to believe it and take steps toward it. It was a daily commitment and sometimes I only had the strength for that one day. Sometimes I refused the strength God offered and made things worse. It was a slow process.

Another powerful passage that I focused on was the famous love chapter, 1 Corinthians 13. Verses 4-7 say,

> *Love is patient, love is kind. It does not envy, it does not boast, it is not proud. It does not dishonor others, it is not self-seeking, it is not easily angered, it keeps no record of wrongs. Love does not delight*

in evil but rejoices with the truth. It always protects, always trusts, always hopes, always perseveres.

It would have been easier at times to give up, close myself off, and move on, but I would have missed out on the deeper work of God within me. God wanted me to love and sacrifice from a place of strength.

Chapter 4
Learning How to Talk Again

*I love being married. It's so great to find that one special person
you want to annoy for the rest of your life.*
~ Rita Rudner

I don't recall how or why it happened, but during the same
season we started feeling hopeful about our marriage again we
began walking our dog, Casey, after dinner. Initially it was no
big deal, just something we enjoyed doing. The kids were old
enough to be on their own for a few minutes, and it felt good to
stretch our legs and watch Casey run. (This was the highlight
of Casey's day, and soon it became ours as well.)

There were several nights we finished dinner, told the kids
they were on dish duty, and headed out (I can still see the
expression on their faces – priceless!) Casey learned the
routine and began looking at us around 7 p.m. as if to say, "Can
we get this show on the road?"

We walked about a mile-and-a-half, and the subdivision next to
our house was newer with big homes, 2 – 3 acre lots, and even
a few open fields. It was a pretty walk, and that made a big
difference. We watched deer scamper through the tall grass,
saw the occasional fox, looked up to see the bats twisting and
turning, and marveled at the pink, orange, and red of a late
summer sky. It was the perfect setting for us, but it was far
more than just nice scenery and a little exercise.

We began to notice that we could talk about some very stressful subjects on these walks that we struggled to discuss in the house, face to face. Along with this realization came the idea to press the envelope and tackle some really difficult topics as we walked. We would still fight sometimes. In fact, we had some knock-down-drag-out arguments a few nights while the bats swooped overhead. But, even when it was hard, we always felt like we were making progress. There was no despair, no hopelessness.

Most nights we were able to connect on a deep level. Those walks were a pathway to healing, hope, and ultimately, oneness.

I don't pretend to fully grasp all of the science and psychology behind why human beings communicate better while walking (or doing other forms of physical activity), but I am a big believer in couples walking and talking several times a week. It is a sacred practice for us now. (Just last night we took a two-mile walk on the beach with our new puppy, Rocky. It's hard for us to imagine our marriage now without this simple discipline.)

One of the reasons walking is so helpful for me is that it helps me relax. I am one of those Type-A personalities who needs to have a clear goal to justify any activity! Walking gives me a goal – we have a starting point and a destination. I can relax because even if the conversation is a total flop, at least we achieved a goal and finished something! (Pray for Sandi, it can't be easy for the poor girl...)

A few other insights we picked up along the way?

- I have learned to ask Sandi this key question: "Are you venting right now, or are you asking me to do something?" If your spouse is an external processor, learn to ask this question early in the conversation – before your blood pressure elevates. Most of the time she just needs to vent, and once I know that I can relax and let her talk as long as she wants. I don't even have to say anything usually. I can just watch the dog and keep taking another step toward our goal; it's a win/win.

- Complain to each other about your kids before confronting them. As we wrestle through the parenting challenges that often accompany the teen years we have felt our share of frustration. We gave each other permission on these walks to get it all off our chest and say out loud just how difficult our kids can be sometimes. (For those of you with perfect children, please put this book down immediately and find the nearest priest so you can confess your sin of lying!) After purging the pent-up angst, we could then talk about the situation and how we needed to respond. It had a cathartic effect and the follow up conversations with our children always went better, and we were far less likely to get triangulated. (Parenting tip: it's okay to NOT respond immediately to your child when they mess up. We simply tell them: "I don't know how I am going to respond to this yet. I will talk it over with mom/dad and we will get back with you.")

- Save the most intense conversations for long walks. This is now our practice. If we have something heavy to talk about, we will put it off (if possible) until our next walk. We have walked in the rain, the snow, and at 11 p.m. There are dynamics at work when walking side by side that lower blood pressure, release certain chemicals in the brain, and decrease stress levels. (There is a large body of research to supports this.)

Now that we were able to communicate at both a heart and head level, what did we need to talk about? For us, there were three monsters under the bed. They were:

1. Does God still have a plan for us?

2. Can we really trust God after surviving ministry and marriage trauma?

3. Will I go back for the girl?

The first monster was whether or not we believed God still had a plan for us. This was a tough one, because cynicism had crept in and we were wary. It was far better to sit in our separate corners of the ring than stand in the middle and hurt each other. But, we knew, that if God had a plan for us we would have to meet in the middle and figure it out together, a significant gut check to be sure.

The other obstacle we faced was our weakened faith in God. Two unresolved questions were eroding our faith:

- If God called us into church planting in the first place why did he abandon us and allow us to struggle so much?

- If taking such a big risk for God brought so much pain the last time, should we do it again?

Verbalizing these questions was our first step. Talking about our fears brought them into the light. Naming our fears gave us a sense of authority over them as they diminished and lost their power within the larger story of our lives. My friends in Al-Anon like to say, "You are only as sick as your secrets." We were sick, but the secret was out and the healing had begun.

Why had God asked us to plant a church? There were the dozens of people who were exposed to the Gospel and began a relationship with Jesus. There were the Christians who developed into leaders and went on to have substantial kingdom impact. And, there was the refining process he was working out in our hearts and relationship. We knew that God refined faith in the same way precious metals are refined. First, they are heated and the dross rises to the top and gets skimmed off. Then, once purified they are combined with harder metals and shaped through the application of more heat and pressure. I already knew all of this. As a matter of fact, I had preached on this passage many times:

In all this you greatly rejoice, though now for a little while you may have had to suffer grief in all kinds of trials. These have come so that the proven genuineness of your faith—of greater worth than gold, which perishes

*even though refined by fire—may result in praise, glory
and honor when Jesus Christ is revealed.* ~ 1 Peter 1:6-7

Yes, God had heated and tested our faith. The impurities were rising to the surface, and some of them were ugly and embarrassing. One thing is for certain; this is not what we signed up for! Apparently God had a different agenda than the one we had in mind when we agreed to go out as church planters. And this became the critical question: "Do we still believe in God's goodness in spite of the sorrow?"

This question of God's goodness took center stage. If we did not believe that deep down our Heavenly Father was good and personally loved and cared for us, we could not move forward. Round and round we walked, and round and round we talked. Here is what we agreed to in the end:

1. The Bible teaches us that God is good, but the Bible also teaches us that God uses trials to shape our faith and character. We trusted God's word and chose to live in the tension of both his goodness and his ultimate goal of conforming us into the image of Christ. This satisfied us intellectually.

2. As we examined our own histories we concluded that for most of our lives we personally experienced the goodness and love of God. Other than my ministry burnout and the marriage struggles it triggered, the testimony of our lives pointed to a good and caring Heavenly Father. We chose to interpret our present circumstances within the larger context of our personal

narratives. This gave us some breathing room emotionally.

3. Finally, we made a decision to act upon what we knew and believed to be true: that God was good, and to wait for our feelings to catch up. This was huge. Had we waited to feel happy and joyful about God before making the decision to follow him, we would still be walking in circles.

So, we decided that yes, God is good (even if we don't feel it right now). This allowed us to move on to the next question: "Can we trust him again?" After all, just because someone is a good person (or even a good Deity) doesn't necessarily mean you can count on him or her when surrounded by the enemy. They may have the best intentions (they may even love you) but are they able to help? Do they have the authority and power to make a difference? Can they deliver?

On August 19, 1989 Sandi and I were married. She was 20, and I had just turned 22. We included Psalm 34:3 on our wedding invitations:

Glorify the LORD with me; let us exalt his name together.

The desire of our hearts was to bring God more glory as a married couple than we could as individuals. We believed he had ordained a unique way for us to exalt his name together. The adventure of marriage was discovering what God had in mind for us, how he wanted to work in and through us. We were up for anything. In fact, just before our engagement I bought a large map of Africa and hung it in my apartment. One night I pointed to that map and told Sandi, in no uncertain terms, that if she wanted to marry me someday we were most likely heading to Africa as missionaries. (Yes, I really said that, and yes, she agreed!)

So, in 1998 when we packed up our house to start a new church in a city we had only visited once it was just another chapter in the grand adventure. Up until that point God has blessed just about everything we touched, so why not?

Ah, but now we were older. Now we were wiser. Now we had the scars to prove that certain ministry assignments are more dangerous than others. Now we knew fear.

We believed that God was good, but was he GREAT? Was God big enough and wise enough and strong enough to heal what was broken while we moved into another missionary adventure? Would we wind up at the same dead end of burnout and relational crisis? And another question: was God attentive enough? Did he really know every hair on our heads? Was he truly involved in the messy details of our lives? Was he going with us personally, or was he just out there somewhere preoccupied with more pressing matters?

Then, on May 5, 2013 it happened. We had been praying, walking, talking, and waiting on God for over three years with no breakthrough. Sandi was still selling technology and traveling more than ever. I was still serving as a church planting director for a denomination, also on the road a couple of nights every week. We were attending a mega-church almost thirty minutes away struggling to find community and our place to serve. We were honestly knocking on every door that presented itself, but could not extract ourselves from the rut we spent the past ten years excavating. We knew that God had something different for us, a way to partner fully in life and ministry that once came so naturally but was now so elusive. But we could not find the way – until May 5, 2013. The events of that day ignited a chain reaction that God used to disrupt the status quo and set us on a new path entirely.

I was visiting one of our church plants that morning. Two things happened during the worship service that shook me to the core. First, I got a text from Sandi that our dog, Casey, had been run over and was paralyzed. She was rushing the dog to the vet, but it didn't look like Casey was going to make it. I was heartbroken. A dam of grief broke loose inside of me that day that flowed for a solid week. I cried every day for Casey, but I also grieved for all that had been lost. Deep down I sensed that God had so much more for us, and that we – no, that I – had squandered the past decade through unfocused anger and unspoken fear. The words of Jesus echoed, *"If you want to save your life, you must first lose it..."*

The second bombshell was internal, underground. It was a rare, out-of-body experience that I have only encountered a few times. As I was sitting there during the worship service I suddenly saw everything as if I were in the back of the room floating ten feet in the air. I saw myself sitting there, I saw the pastor up front doing his very best, and I saw a small group of people seated in plastic chairs trying to put a happy face on a tough reality. What tough reality? This church plant was probably not going to make it. The tougher reality? This beautiful family that invested so deeply to start the church was heading into a season of deep grief and deeper disillusionment. I knew it all too well.

And I was the one who put them there.

Click. "Never again. I can never do this again."

I drove home that afternoon, found Casey lying on the front lawn with our daughter Emily, paralyzed from the neck down. It was without a doubt one of the most pitiful sights I have ever beheld. Early the next morning we brought all the kids into the living room to say goodbye to Casey, and I took her back to the vet. She died in my arms a few minutes later. (To this day I can't talk about this without tears.)

Grieving for Casey, but also for that young family pouring their lives into a church plant that was likely to leave them beaten and bloodied, I told Sandi, "I can't do this anymore. I can't keep sending these young families into the trenches equipped to start worship services but not prepared to make disciples." It felt like I had been sending our best and brightest recruits to the front lines with slingshots to engage machine guns and tanks. It was reckless. I was conscience stricken.

Two weeks later I spoke with my boss. I was completely honest with him, knowing full well it meant walking away from my ministry position and a full time income (and from a group of people I loved and respected, especially him). I told him; "Until God shows me a different way to plant churches, I can't keep doing this." I still believed in the church, and in church planting, but there was something essential missing in my leadership and strategy. Until I could discover what that was and gain confidence that our church planting efforts grew from the soil of disciple making, I had to step away. And not just for my own sake (although I did have to look in the mirror everyday), but also for the sake of those pastors and families who were being sacrificed for a counterfeit system. It was just wrong.

My job was coming to an end. I had nothing else lined up. What were we going to do?

Our road turns southward

It just so happens that a leadership coaching and training organization based in South Carolina had asked Sandi and me to come down and serve an apprenticeship. This was not a job offer; there was no paycheck. But it was an opportunity to step away from leading for a season and focus on learning. And I knew I needed to go back to the drawing board and learn. The name of the group was 3DM.

I felt compelled to go for it. But, how could we survive financially? I had no job, and my best prospects were to do some long distance coaching and go back to my painting profession. If Sandi quit her job and we both had to start over (with our oldest daughter heading off to college), I feared it was just too much. And then, Sandi came home from work one day and said her employer would allow her to work remote for ten months. She could keep her job and we could make the move to South Carolina, at least theoretically.

Fast-forward thirty days. We found a great family to rent our house in Michigan, Sandi was approved to work remote, and 3DM wanted us to come down. The door was open, but could we really do this? Could we take our 14-year-old son, and our

16-year-old daughter and move 850 miles away? Could we leave our oldest daughter in Michigan to start college? Could we leave my parents, my sick father, and Sandi's mom behind?

This was the most intense, gut wrenching decision we ever had to make. Sandi was frozen with guilt over moving so far from Megan and our parents. My father's health was deteriorating rapidly, and he would pass away later that fall. It was the closest I have ever felt to what Abraham must have experienced as he placed Isaac on that altar and raised the knife. It was a desperate situation.

In the end, it was exactly that sense of desperation that compelled me to risk it all and take the plunge. Why was I so desperate? Because Sandi and I had been stuck for too many years not living out the life I knew God had for us. I wanted my wife back. I wanted our marriage back. I wanted a partner by my side to do life and ministry with. And I was willing to pay a heavy price.

The moment of truth came one evening at *Olive Garden*. It was time to make a decision – were we making the move or not? Sandi was resistant. She could not overcome the guilt. I was frustrated. This was the best opportunity that had come along in over ten years, and I felt certain God wanted us to take it. The conversation became animated, people sitting nearby munching on their unlimited breadsticks looked over at us with raised eyebrows.

I had learned to respect Sandi's "no". This could only work for us if she, under no compulsion or pressure from me, said "yes".

She not only had to agree with me, she had to do so freely. So, I took a deep breath and in a calm voice asked this question:

"Will you follow me?"

She had a choice to make, and it was her choice. She was either willing to follow me to South Carolina for an opportunity at a fresh start or she wasn't. I would submit to whatever she decided and accept it as God's will. I chose partnership over control.

I was going back for the girl. She was more important to me than my job. She was more important to me than living in Michigan near family. She was more important to me than the comfort or wishes of our children. I was choosing us, and I was asking her to follow me. Yes, it looked crazy. Yes, it felt irresponsible. Yes, we were going to make a lot of people we loved really mad at us. But none of that mattered to me in that moment. I just wanted the girl to be with me. (I know, incredibly sappy, but completely true.)

Sandi's expression changed. She softened. You could see the stress and tension melt from her face. She said:

"Yes, I will follow you."

Roll the credits. They moved to South Carolina and lived happily ever after. Well, sort of...

Research on effects of exercise and communication:

Spark: The Revolutionary New Science of Exercise and the Brain (Paperback, January 1, 2013) by John J. Ratey and Eric Hagerman

Wright, Suzanne. "Walk and Talk Therapy." *WebMD*. WebMD, 1 Apr. 2008. Web. <http://www.webmd.com/balance/features/walk-and-talk-therapy>. Exercise is good for the body and the mind. It may improve psychotherapy sessions, too.

From Sandi

"Now faith is the substance of things hoped for, the evidence of things not seen." (Hebrews 11:1)

"We walk by faith and not by sight." (2 Corinthians 5:7)

Some days I felt as though I was setting myself up for more hurt but each day I would ask God to keep my heart soft and my mind set on·His glory.

We experienced breakthrough when we started walking regularly after dinner. There were several times when we walked in silence and it took a while before some of the barriers started to come down. We tested the waters with some safer topics first and slowly graduated to more difficult things. I still spoke in respectful ways on these walks and continued to work on my own boundaries. I didn't use every walk as an opportunity to complain but I also wasn't afraid to disagree or share my dissatisfaction if the topic came up. After a while I felt safe enough to share some hopes and expectations. The conversations started to shift away from fixing current problems to moving forward to a better future together.

I often think about why walking was such a lifesaver for our marriage. Yes it was good exercise and got Tom and I outside with our dog, and yes it has been proven that some people can connect better while walking, but I think there are other reasons, too. Walking taught me some discipline in my communication. It forced me to wait to talk about certain topics instead of bringing them up anytime and

---

anywhere. No wonder Tom was always on edge because I could hit him with a negative conversation at any moment. Walking created a boundary for starting and ending the potentially stressful conversations. It was almost like scheduling a meeting that had a starting and ending time. Any topic was free game during the scheduled time, but we knew that the meeting would end soon, so we worked hard and stayed focused until the end. It gave me hope that we would eventually talk about the important stuff, but helped me to be patient until a walk to bring it up.

So, while we were successfully talking about difficult subjects on our walks, we were equally successful at making other family times more positive and less stressful. This reduced the tension from meals, bedtimes, dates, and activities because I didn't always wonder about when we might get a chance to talk. Just like writing and emailing our thoughts to each other slowed me down and helped contain the conversation, walking was a positive way to bring structure and boundaries to our verbal communication. Tom was loving and patient with me as I learned how to communicate in this effective, contained way.

The primary topic of discussion for over a month on our walks was Tom's ministry at the church we planted and his desire to make a change. He wanted to work with integrity and serve God in a way that powerfully advanced the Kingdom. This topic had often been a struggle because Tom's gifts and desires didn't always seem to align with mine; my insecurities turned the conversations to my needs instead of Tom's heartfelt desires. I thought that Tom's ideas might make my life more difficult and I was afraid to engage with them. I wanted the title of pastor's wife and relied on the position to bring me identity and credibility. So for me, it was a really big deal to set aside my hopes and dreams of us leading a church together and talk about other ministry options.

You know the story, Tom did resign from his leadership position at Lighthouse and we eventually started attending a large church about twenty minutes away. It was a great move overall for our family and on good days I could see God's grace and healing. On the bad days I felt like I was in a holding pattern and just had to wait until the next thing. I kept thinking of King David. He was told that he would be king, yet spent many years running from Saul and hiding in caves before it happened. He held onto a promise but had to wait until God's timing to bring it to fruition. I also thought of the story of Joseph in Genesis. He had dreams of greatness, but instead got sold into slavery and spent years in prison before God started using him in the ways he promised.

I felt like I was in a cave, waiting.

Recently I heard the word trust defined as "carelessness". My first reaction to this definition was negative. I don't like the word careless, but the more I thought about it, the more it made sense. Total trust means that I can proceed without fear, knowing that God cares for me (so I can care less).

Fast-forward a bit and we got invited to train with a ministry organization called 3DM in the spring of 2013. Moving south became a primary topic of conversation on our walks. Could this be the opportunity to re-engage in ministry partnership with Tom? Was God going to give me a new platform to speak into the lives of pastors and families across the country? I was excited but very scared. There was a whole lot riding on this decision and it would impact not only us but also our children and extended families. I wanted to believe but I just couldn't get myself to take that leap of faith when my trust in Tom and God was still in such a healing mode.

There was something else going on in my life that God used to develop my faith. I was born with a heart condition called a VSD (ventricular septal defect). The bottom line is that I have a hole in my heart and it has never been surgically repaired. Each year I go to the doctor and they run a bunch of tests and tell me that everything is fine and I can go home. In February of 2013 I went in for my regular appointment and it was a very different story. The doctor saw something on my test results that alarmed him. Without going into too much detail, I had a big health scare!

Based on these initial test results, I either had a debilitating health problem or needed open heart surgery. I met with a surgeon and discussed options and spent about three weeks waiting for more information. I was anxious and full of fear. Thankfully, after going to a specialist, I found out that everything was actually fine. I could go on with life as usual -no surgery needed and no disease detected. (Praise God!).

This health scare caused me to evaluate my faith and my commitment to God. It gave me a deeper sense of urgency because my time on this earth could be short. You never know what tomorrow holds and I didn't want to waste it being afraid. Tom expressed so much love and compassion to me during this scary time and it made us both realize how much we truly appreciated each other. Seeing Tom weep over me was very moving. I vowed to obey God and serve him with courageous obedience. I never want to look back at my life and see that I chose fear over faith.

So that was the faith climate going on in my life during that period. It all came down to our dinner conversation at Olive Garden. As Tom wrote in the chapter, the conversation got tense and he was getting impatient. I was still so unsure! Tom finally looked me in the eyes and asked me to follow him. To this day I don't know if the decision to go was right or wrong, but I knew clearly that God gave me a beautiful opportunity to take a huge risk of faith to support my husband. In that moment it became less about the decision to move and more about respecting my husband and obeying God in a tangible way. I believe that God used that "risking it all to follow God and Tom" decision to unlock deeper healing and build momentum. Honestly, it could have been any decision, but God used this to shake things up for us, put us on the same page, and helped us to move forward in faith, hand in hand.

To this day I continue to wrestle with our decision to move to South Carolina. There have been losses and a lot of grief. As I struggle through this season I keep coming back to the same commitment – "I choose us".

Chapter 5
Carrying Loads and Sharing Burdens

"Carry each other's burdens, and in this way you will fulfill the law of Christ."
~ Galatians 6:2

"...each one should carry their own load."
~ Galatians 6:5

Burdens and loads. Sandi and I still had a lot to learn about taking responsibility for ourselves, and when to step in to help each other. The writing of Drs. Cloud and Townsend once again lifted us over a hurdle.

In their book, *Boundaries*, they reflect on these passages from Galatians 6 and write:

> *We are responsible to others and for ourselves...Many times others have "burdens" that are too big to bear. They do not have enough strength, resources, or knowledge to carry the load, and they need help. Denying ourselves to do for others what they cannot do for themselves is showing the sacrificial love of Christ...This is being responsible "to."*

> *On the other hand, verse 5 says that "each one should carry his own load." Everyone has responsibilities that only he or she can carry. These things are our own*

particular "load" that we need to take daily responsibility for and work out...

Problems arise when people act as if their "boulders" are daily loads, and refuse help, or as if their "daily loads" are boulders they shouldn't have to carry. The results of these two instances are either perpetual pain or irresponsibility.[2]

My biggest problem? I wanted to take Sandi's load and her burdens! I wanted to be the hero. I *needed* to be the hero. Along the way I made myself responsible for something that was on her side of the boundary line, something only she could own – her feeling of happiness.

Ironically, the price you pay by taking on someone's load is the inability to help with his or her burdens. You also rob them of the opportunity to learn how to carry their own load. But, this wasn't obvious at first. In fact, this is the kind of response I got from most people:

"Isn't Tom a great guy?"

"Look at how hard he is working for his marriage and his family!"

"God has really blessed the Blaylock family!"

Things looked great on the surface for a long time, but we were both starting to feel the strain a few years into our church

---

[2] Cloud, Henry and John Townsend. *Boundaries*, (Grand Rapids, MI: Zondervan Publishing House, 1992) page 30.

plant. By the time I resigned I was so emotionally depleted that I simply gave up. I quit attempting to carry Sandi's loads, and I quit helping with her burdens. She was on her own emotionally.

Looking back now I see this principle: *When you attempt to carry a person's load, you not only lose energy to help with their burdens, but you also fail to take responsibility for your own stuff.*

I failed to take responsibility for my own feelings of contentment and significance. Instead of finding what I needed through my relationship with Christ, I looked to Sandi's happiness and the success of our church plant to "make" me feel content and important. I resented Sandi for not being happy. I resented God for not turning our church plant into a wild success story. Like Adam, instead of taking responsibility for myself, I said, "This woman you gave me is the real problem."

As God brought healing into our relationship and we began to appreciate the distinction between being responsible *to* one another and not *for* one another, good things happened. A few examples:

1. My stress level decreased dramatically when I stepped back onto my side of the boundary line and no longer felt responsible for Sandi's happiness. As my stress level diminished, so did my anger and resentment. It was a huge weight lifted from our marriage.

2. Sandi stepped up and became more responsible for her own load. She grew in her assertiveness and in her

confidence. The word "no" was firmly rooted in her vocabulary, which enabled her to truly say "yes" with freedom.

3. With most of the frustration gone, I began feeling compassion for Sandi and for her burdens. I realized how negligent I had been and repented of my sin. For a few years I refused to help carry her burdens, and I confessed that to her and asked for forgiveness.

4. Sandi viewed a partnership with me in marriage and ministry as something desirable again. She shifted from feeling emotionally abandoned to seeing me as a partner and ally who could be trusted. She lowered her defenses and chose to follow my leadership again.

5. I was freed up to see how I failed to take ownership for my own load. And I also had the energy to do something about it. My feelings of contentment and significance had been held hostage to things beyond my control. I was now able to come to God personally with these needs and find what I was looking for in my relationship with Christ.

Please understand, this was a long process. This took a few years to work through, and to be honest, and we still have bad days. It was a two-step forward, one-step backward kind of journey. It still is to this day.

A special word to wives

I feel compelled to say something to all the wives reading this book; your husband desperately needs to know that you believe in him, that you are with him, and that you respect him. I realize that sometimes we push you away and make it very difficult for you to communicate these things, but never doubt the impact you have on us.

I went through a very dark season when I honestly believed Sandi made a mistake marrying me, and that she would have been better off marrying someone else. (But, now she was stuck with me and had to make the best of it.) I was still feeling responsible for her happiness at that time, and I knew it was beyond me. I saw myself as a complete failure.

Sandi felt abandoned by me. Practically speaking, she was on her own as I only gave her precious little emotional support. Sandi felt like she had to make all of the important decisions in her life and for our family as I withdrew into myself. I think she reached the place of emotional numbness and just did what she had to do.

The flip side of that scenario is I felt like I had lost my wife. The woman I chose to share life with was no longer there. There was no partnership. There was no intimacy. We were going through the motions of marriage and doing our best to raise three kids. And it grieved me. My own sense of loss created a feeling of indignation inside of me, a sense that this was all wrong and had to be made right. It was that sense of brokenness (along with owning my significant contribution) that eventually grew into a heart-felt conviction. My conviction deepened and became a godly discontent. In the end, this deep-seated discontent drove me to seek breakthrough for our marriage behind any door that looked promising.

It was that search that led us to Pawleys Island, South Carolina.

On August 15, 2013 we packed up our van and SUV and made the fifteen-hour drive from Michigan to Pawleys Island. It was brutal. We arrived at the condo we were renting around midnight and collapsed. The next day we began unpacking. The heat was so intense that the metal on the van would burn bare skin. "How do these people stand this heat?" I wondered to myself.

A week later both kids were attending the local high school, our daughter in Michigan was in college, Sandi was working remote from our bedroom, and I was trying to find some painting work. My dad was really sick, and my mom was very unhappy with me for leaving them behind. It was a stressful and anxious time.

Instead of living happily ever after, we struggled mightily that first year. Grant was angry with us for making him move. My father passed away in November. Sandi cried herself to sleep several nights worrying about Megan and feeling guilty for moving so far away from her and our parents. Moving to South Carolina was the single most difficult transition we have ever made as a family. And yes, there were many times when it felt like a terrible decision. I asked Sandi to trust me, to follow my leadership. Had I made a huge mistake?

In spite of the many challenges, I never believed moving to South Carolina was a mistake. On our darkest days I clung to the following:

- We moved here to get a fresh start in our marriage – we needed to get out of a deep rut and this was the door God opened. We referred to this as our "reset".

- I needed to retool as a spiritual leader. I had led as far as I was able, and it was time to stop leading and start learning. The opportunity with 3DM was the best thing that had come along in several years.

- Our daughter, Emily, was thriving. Almost immediately she found a great group of friends and began growing as a disciple and a leader. She found opportunity and relationship in South Carolina that simply didn't exist for her in Michigan.

Another affirmation was the way these challenges brought us together instead of pulling us apart. For the most part we locked shields and faced whatever life threw at us as a team. In January of 2014 we decided to accept job offers from 3DM and spent nine months working in the same office. In June of that year we sold our house in Michigan and bought a home in Pawleys Island.

How did we remain united and choose faith over fear against so many obstacles? We had hope. Hope that God wasn't finished with us yet. Hope that his good plan would yet unfold in our lives. Hope that the trials our children were experiencing would stretch and grow their faith and character in the long run. Hope that I was getting my wife back, and that we were getting our marriage back. Hope is a powerful and precious thing. Ask anyone who no longer has it…

We also felt hope that God was healing some deep wounds in our hearts individually and as a couple. For Sandi the numbness was gone, which meant she once again felt both pain and joy. We took many long walks on the beach that first year talking about anything and everything. We didn't have any close friends; we only had each other – in retrospect that was part of God's provision.

We learned something that first year that will stay with us always: before you can have oneness, you first must have two-ness.

> *For this reason a man will leave his father and mother and be united to his wife, and the two will become one flesh. So they are no longer two, but one flesh. Therefore what God has joined together, let no one separate.*
> *~ Mark 10:7-9*

It's easy to miss, but before you can have one you must first have two. In other words, before two people can form a new identity as a fully integrated married couple, there must first be two healthy, functioning, interdependent (better yet, God-dependent) people.

If one partner looks to the other to complete him or her, the marriage is headed for trouble. I wanted to complete Sandi by taking ownership of something that wasn't mine, and it undermined my respect for her and our ability to find oneness.

I also believed Sandi would complete me. She would be the distressed damsel and I would be the shimmering knight. I needed her to need me, and if I could save the day I would be complete.

Only healthy people who respect their boundaries and the boundaries of others can truly experience this kind of oneness. Why? Because it is a joining together of two whole people. It is the merging of two equals who learn to partner, love, and submit to one another. It is the culmination of two lives that have been redeemed and filled to overflowing with the love and grace of God.

Turns out the Hollywood ideal of finding a soul mate to complete you is a cheap counterfeit compared to what God intends for Christian marriage. (Shouldn't this be obvious as we read the tabloid headlines at the grocery store?)

Something occurred to me during our first year in South Carolina that I somehow had missed; I could never fulfill the calling that God had on my life without Sandi's help and active engagement.

After the dust cleared and I could once again see just what God was asking me to do, I realized I couldn't do it by myself. It was too big. It required gifts and skills that I didn't possess. The journey was too long and too dangerous to embark on alone.

What did this mean? How could I communicate this to Sandi after all we had been through?

I simply came to her one day and said this:

I can't do what God has asked me to do by myself. I need your help. Will you help me?

Her "yes" to that question transported us into a new reality. It was no longer about how to heal a broken marriage; it was now about how to step into our calling together. The focus shifted from a marriage on the mend to a marriage on mission. And that made all the difference.

From Sandi

While Tom worked on his issues, I had to take ownership for my lack of boundaries. Until I respected myself enough to say, "no" and voice my own opinions, I was never going to have Tom's respect. At times during this process I was angry that I had to distance myself from Tom and the support I felt like I deserved as his wife. "Why did I have to change and pretend that I was okay with doing things independently? Why didn't God give me someone who was more like me?" I was immature and I resisted growing up. I had relied on Tom too long to carry my burdens and loads, and I resented him for refusing to help with either one anymore. I remember telling the counselor that I felt like I was standing alone and naked in front of a stadium full of people laughing at me, including Tom. This season of our marriage was discouraging and lonely.

"I am reading the Boundaries in Marriage book. God is speaking to me through this book that I need to be a complete person apart from Tom and bring my "wholeness" to the marriage to make it better. I need to value and take ownership of my feelings, desires, and behaviors. I need to celebrate and grow in who God has made me to be. I need to be courageous to do this. I also need to realize and respect how God has made Tom. Boundaries says I can't control his behavior, so the courage part I need is to obey God, respect my boundaries, and trust God with how Tom views me.

I read in the Boundaries book on page 81:

"As you become more defined by your own boundaries, you will experience your mate's feelings and decisions as having more to do with him than with you. This will free you to allow him to be free"

I want this, but it makes me scared.

I have given Tom the power to control me because I am such a people pleaser. I have tried for many years to be the type of person that Tom wants and respects. I understand that instead I should be working hard to please God - not man. It has been (and still is) a confusing line. I struggle with my role as supportive/submissive wife (so I become what I think Tom wants - that is not being true to who God made me. I can't become someone I am not - so I feel like a failure and the cycle continues.) I'm at the point where I do not want to continue the cycle. I trust and pray that as I become more and more who God wants me to be that God will bring healing instead of division in our marriage.

I need to move on in some respects and not look to Tom as the final judge of goodness and character. To be honest that scares me and it makes me feel like I am giving up hope of "oneness" with him - but I understand that this thinking is part of my problem. Oneness does not mean "sameness". I don't know if I will ever get the respect/affirmation that I want from Tom because who I am and what I

> *represent is not what I think Tom respects. I will move on and look to God and other "safe" groups of friends for that. If God chooses to bless me with a spouse who can see things and appreciate things from my perspective, then great. If not, I trust God and love Tom anyway."*

~ Sandi's journal entry, August 30, 2007

I was growing and getting stronger. Tom watched this growth, which encouraged him to start helping me when appropriate. He knew I wasn't counting on him for everything, so it became safe for him to re-engage with me. He wasn't feeling cornered or trapped anymore. We both started taking responsibility for our own feelings, while being responsible to each other.

So we planned a move to South Carolina.

The most difficult thing about moving to South Carolina was being far away from our daughter Megan who was 18 years old at the time. I desperately wanted her to move with us but felt like I couldn't impose that decision on her. She didn't know anyone in SC and wanted to stick with her plan of attending a school in Michigan. I also really struggled moving so far away from my mom and Tom's parents. I felt guilty and cried myself to sleep on more than one occasion. I'm so thankful for that night at Olive Garden when God took the pressure off of me about the decision to move. If I had made the decision thinking it was the best and wisest plan, then I might have doubted my ability to make any decision in the future. Knowing that I moved out of faith and obedience to God and respect for Tom allowed me to trust that it was right, regardless of how difficult it felt at the time.

Packing up our home in Michigan was really hard. I had so many good memories in that home of raising our children, planting Lighthouse Church, ministering to friends, and hosting multiple gatherings. I walked into each room and allowed the memories to flood in and was completely overcome by thanksgiving for how God had provided for each need. I ran my fingers over the growth chart marks on our son's bedroom wall before we painted over them. I raised my hands in the air in each room and prayed that God would use the lessons learned and the prayers of faith spoken there over the years for his glory. I prayed that God would bless the buyers and use our home as a blessing to many. I'm not usually that sentimental about things, but I really lost it as I said goodbye to that house. It represented an era for me that I was thankful for, but also one I was ready to leave behind.

It represented God's grace.

Instead of fear, I chose the better thing of moving and trusting to partner with Tom again in ministry. The outcome or success didn't matter as much as the decision to follow.

Tom needed to see my willingness.

It was time to admit that I was the one who felt stuck in my job and did nothing to change it. I could no longer hold onto the false belief that Tom was the reason I didn't have ministry choices. Not everyone will be called to move to a new state, but for me it was the very thing that gave us a new level of partnership and commitment. It was a way for me to say "yes".

Proverbs 31:12 says, "She brings him good, not harm, all the days of her life".

It was clear to me that the way I could do my husband good and not harm was to believe in him and trust him. I empowered him to lead regardless and it was a beautiful thing.

Chapter 6
The Choice: Going Fast Alone or Going Far Together?

"Love does not consist of gazing at each other, but in looking outward together in the same direction."
– Antoine de Saint-Exupery, Airman's Odyssey

I will never forget the first time I heard it. I was sitting in a Fort Wayne, Indiana boardroom. I recall settling in for a very long meeting and scanning the table for snacks (hoping for dark chocolate).

Our leader, (then Regional Director Steve Jones who currently serves as the President of the Missionary Church) made the following statement:

There is an old African proverb that says: "If you want to go fast, go alone. But if you want to go far, go together."

Click.

Time slowed down for me as I took this in. In an instant God had my full, undivided attention and I knew he was sending a message through Steve.

Here was the message:

"Tom, in your headlong pursuit to plant more churches and accomplish greater and greater things for me, you have left

Sandi behind. Go back for her. I am sending you to a place of blessing and impact, but you can only make this journey with her at your side."

I don't recall another word uttered the rest of that day. I was transfixed on the image of leaving my wife behind. I knew it was true, and it grieved me. Rising up beneath the grief was a sense of urgency. "I have to go back for her! I hope it's not too late!"

The year was 2011. This was one of the catalytic events God used to reshape my life and our marriage. It came during that period of long walks while waiting on God to open doors. And this message became a key that would open many doors. Going far together would bring breakthrough, we just didn't know how yet.

But, first things first; why did I leave Sandi behind to begin with?

It was the book, *Covenant and Kingdom* by Mike Breen that helped me understand this better. Mike makes a compelling argument for two strands of DNA that run throughout all scripture: covenant and kingdom. Covenant is all about relationship and two people becoming one, new identity. God's covenant with Abram illustrates the power of this bonding. Abram's name change to Abraham signified the intimacy of covenant as he took on part of God's name (just like Sandi's name changed through our covenant of marriage). It is through covenant that we receive our truest identity.

Kingdom, on the other hand, speaks of responsibility, authority, and power. When we engage God's kingdom the dead rise, the earth splits, and mountains blaze. If covenant is a romance novel, kingdom is a fast paced, action packed thriller.

My problem? I was attempting to earn my identity through kingdom accomplishments. My bigger problem? Since God gives identity *by his grace* through covenantal relationships, I was searching in the wrong place. Believing I had to somehow earn my identity I always felt compelled to do more. As I moved from one thing to the next in a restless pursuit of identity and affirmation, Sandi grew weary and wounded.

This was our exact situation after I resigned from our first church plant. Sandi was deeply wounded, and my sense of identity and significance were threatened by my apparent lack of success in leading our church to greater heights. I needed another win, and I needed it quickly. So, we planted another church. This time we used a house church model, which meant I also needed to find employment. Hey, another opportunity to earn my identity! Why not start a new business to fund our church plant and pay the bills for our family? Great idea!

Let's be clear about one thing; I was in no way, shape, or form ready to plant another church. I, too, was deeply wounded, but I didn't feel like I had the time to address all of that. In fact, I was emotionally, physically, and mentally exhausted. Sandi was reeling from all of the broken and strained relationships that were left in the wake of my resignation. It was the worst possible time to attempt another church plant. Yet, I felt driven to do so.

That's when I left Sandi behind. That's when she got out and I drove off. She could not follow me. She tried her best to be supportive, but it just wasn't in her. Instead of leading her into a season of rest and healing focused upon our covenant with God, one another, and the friends who loved us I pushed her back into an ill-conceived attempt to plant another church.

But, it gets worse. I began viewing Sandi as a liability. She couldn't keep up with me anymore. Her need to slow down and find healing through relationship and a grace filled community felt like a weakness to me. My attitude became, "Get over it already and help me build this new church. Don't you know that people are going to hell?"

Once again, failure was not an option. Once again, our marriage paid a heavy price. And, once again, I justified my sinful attitudes toward Sandi and my striving for something God had already given me (identity as a beloved son) through spiritual sounding logic.

Maybe now you can appreciate what was happening in my heart while sitting in that boardroom. God was calling me back to that fork in the road. He was transporting me back in time to those raw days following my burnout as a church planter. But this time, instead of allowing my fear of failure dictate my response to all of that hurt and loss, I was given the opportunity to choose another path. This time I would embrace covenant before kingdom. This time I would cling to Sandi as we mourned the loss together. This time I would find my true identity in all that Christ accomplished for me. I was *already* pleasing in God's sight!

I was finally ready. Christ promised to build his church; I didn't need to carry that burden. God was calling me to covenant faithfulness that began with him and then Sandi. Before embarking on the next kingdom exploit I first needed to be washed afresh in the grace of covenant. I needed to put the car in reverse, go back to that fork in the road, open the passenger door and ask my wife to come back in.

Here are some of the tangible ways Sandi has come back into relationship and partnership with me:

- In 2012 she entered into a coaching relationship with me. She joined me every Friday morning as we learned how to more faithfully pattern our lives after Jesus and how to lead others to do the same.

- She invested with me. We invested $100 per month to bring her into that coaching relationship. We made a decision to invest some of our treasure (time and money) into our own growth. (Do not underestimate the importance of this step!)

- She followed me to South Carolina, in spite of her fears and doubts.

- She quit two good jobs, took huge pay cuts, and made space in her life and schedule to re-engage our relationship.

- We are now sharing with others both our story and some of the principles of this book in a variety of settings.

Speaking of principles, here is one God has emblazoned on my forehead:

Covenant faithfulness precedes kingdom fruitfulness.

Not only does it precede it, I believe it also empowers and over the long haul perpetuates it.

The dangers of trying to make kingdom ministry happen outside of covenant are many. One of our coaches, Eric Pheiffer, shared the following illustration with us over lunch in 2012:

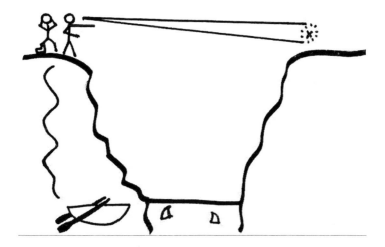

This illustrates what Paul said in Ephesians 4:11–12:

> "So Christ himself gave the apostles, the prophets, the evangelists, the pastors and teachers, to equip his people for works of service, so that the body of Christ may be built up..."

Standing high on the mountain we see the apostle. Next to him - pulling her hair out in frustration - is the apostle's wife. (I say "wife" because this was clearly a parable intended for Sandi and me.)

If you notice, you will see that she is not well. In fact, her foot is in a cast. Seems as though her loving husband has been dragging her through some rough terrain at full speed for a long time. She is wounded, but he doesn't seem to notice. His attention is elsewhere. He has tunnel vision for that next goal over the river and on top that distant mountain. He sees this goal in high definition, and to him it has already become very real (at times more real than the woman standing right in front of him).

Can you feel the tension between our stick figures? He is ready to jump into shark-infested waters and plans to bring her along (kicking and screaming if necessary). He sees anything less as a half-hearted compromise. The shortest distance between two points is a straight line. This is all the logic he needs.

Can you hear what she is trying to say to him?

First she is pleading, "I am hurt and I need time to heal. Will you wait for me? Will you help me? After I regain my strength we can climb that mountain together."

But, she is also saying, "Look, there is another way to do this. I see a boat near the river, and we can use it to cross over. It will take more time, but we will avoid the sharks and get there safely."

How does an immature apostle respond to this honest, reasonable, and helpful input from his wife? I did three things:

1. Ignore her and hope she simply gets on board with the next mission

2. Guilt her into submission by pointing out how desperately God needs us to do this

3. Shut her down with anger, and if she still isn't agreeable dive in without her

Is it any wonder Sandi quit following me? Not only was she wounded, but I wasn't a leader worth following. In fact, I had become reckless. Her covenant with me no longer felt safe to her. Emotionally she began backing away while I was all the more driven to push ahead. The result was a deep disconnect. We were no longer two who had become one. Our reality? We lived as two separate people who happened to be married. An intruder had crept into our covenant and driven a wedge in the heart of our oneness. And I opened the door.

Do you see the path of alienation we were on? Can you appreciate why we have so much passion to tell our story, which is really His story of grace and redemption? Do you feel a spark of hope rising up in your soul for your own marriage?

So, whether you see yourself as a pastor, evangelist, or apostle it really doesn't matter. We all bring strengths and weaknesses into our marriages. We're all susceptible to intruders. Christian marriages are under attack and too many are decaying from within.

And yet, there is hope. If you have read this far you must care about your marriage. You probably have a desire for God to bless others through your partnership, starting with your family and expanding out. Maybe you feel stuck right now, or maybe you have lost the reality of oneness and wonder if you can ever get it back.

If you are feeling disconnected, how do you turn things around? Here are four practical steps you can start taking today:

1. Own you own stuff

No matter how difficult or unresponsive your spouse may be, embrace the truth that it begins with you. There are two crucial steps we take to own our own stuff:

1. First, we relinquish the illusion of control that we have (or wish we had) over our spouse.

Cloud and Townsend write in *Boundaries in Marriage*:

> "We have no power over the attitudes and actions of other people. We can't make our spouse grow up. We can't stop our spouse from exhibiting a troublesome habit or character flaw. We can't force our spouse to come home on time for dinner, to refrain from yelling at us, or to initiate conversation with us. The fruit of the Spirit is self-control, not other-control (Galatians 5:23). God himself does not exercise such power over us, even though he could (2 Peter 3:9)."

Letting go of that fantasy of control may be the most difficult hurdle for you to overcome. For me, it felt like the death of a dear friend! This is a part of my sinful nature that I must die to every day. Only those who can confess: "There is a God, and I am not him!" can find real freedom here.

2. Take responsibility for what you can control

OK, so we all agree (at least intellectually) that we can't control other people. As we let go of that pursuit we discover more energy to invest in those things we do have some control over.

Again, Cloud and Townsend:

> *"If you don't have power to change your spouse, what do you have power over? You have the power to confess, submit, and repent of your own hurtful ways in your marriage. You can identify these hurtful ways, ask God for his help to overcome them, and be willing to change."*

It was only after Sandi saw me taking ownership of my own problems and flaws that she stopped protecting herself and moved towards me. As I became safe and supportive again she lowered the walls and we moved back into relationship.

Jesus said to remove the beam out of your own eye before attempting to remove the speck out of another's eye. There is no relationship where this truth is more powerfully on display than marriage.

2. *Find rest in the identity Christ gives you*

The most loving and helpful thing you can ever do for your spouse is to renounce every idol in your life.

Whatever you look to for identity, other than God, is an idol. You may look to the idols of success, ministry effectiveness, your child's achievement, or your bank account to define who you are. If so, then they are all idols to you.

Exodus 20:3 says, *"You shall have no other gods before me."* The passage goes on to describe God as "jealous". The simple truth is that God is the greatest, most glorious, most loving, and most gracious reality in existence. When you place something in front of him it arouses his jealousy, and his compassion. We arouse his jealousy because he will not allow a counterfeit to take his rightful place in our affections; we arouse his compassion because he knows that all idolatry leads to bondage and heartbreak.

As Christians our identity comes from who God says that we are. We submit to God's definition of reality as a more reliable authority than how we feel or what others may say or think about us. As a follower of Jesus, who are you?

According to God's word you are:

- God's child
- Loved
- Forgiven
- Accepted
- Righteous
- Empowered
- Gifted

- Spirit-filled

- Authorized

- Sent

You are a unique reflection of his image, his glory. And when you and your spouse live into his purposes for your marriage his glory is multiplied.

3. Make the right investments

Over the last two years we have invested thousands of dollars into a boat, a truck for our son, college for our oldest daughter, and I am now scheming ways to afford a big hunting trip out west next year.

We invest time and money into the things we care about.

So, how much time and money have you invested into your marriage recently?

Let me ask another question; how do you feel about investing in your marriage? If the prospect of pouring time and money into your marriage makes you feel discouraged or anxious, that could be a sign that hope is waning. We invest in things we believe will bring a return. However, when hope is weak we are no longer motivated to keep investing. Instead, we slip into the habit of benign neglect (or worse). Our energy shifts to keeping the peace as we look to other people or things to fill the void.

These were the investments we made that brought the greatest return:

1. The book, *101 Nights of Grrreat Romance* and the commitment to find a baby sitter and start dating again on a regular basis. (This is where the turnaround started for us – after several years of little to no investment.)

2. A special 15-year anniversary trip to Mackinac Island (Sandi worked hard to make this trip memorable for us)

3. A weekly coaching relationship we entered together

4. Personal Christian counseling (for me) and then marriage counseling for us

5. The discipline of walking after dinner

6. Moving to South Carolina in order to reset our marriage and ministry

7. Praying together every night before going to sleep

Please listen to this: you will have a better chance of success if you start with something small and simple.

If Sandi would have come to me four years ago and demanded to move out of state for the sake of resetting our marriage, I would have fought her every step of the way. Neither one of us were ready for that much change and commitment.

Instead, she came home one night with a book, and asked if I would be willing to give it a try. Honestly, the cover of the book led me to believe it might boost our love life, so I agreed.

It was our first baby step.

What happens when you keep taking baby steps? Pretty soon you look around and realize that you have moved to a new place (sometimes literally).

So, whether it's a book, a marriage retreat, or something bigger like counseling, pray for wisdom on the best place to begin. Sandi had the insight to draw me out of my shell through the right question at the right time. Her patience and humility eventually paid off.

4. Pray for breakthrough (and look for the grace)

I mentioned a moment ago that Sandi and I pray together every night before going to sleep (when I am not on the road and we are sleeping in the same zip code, that is). That may not sound like a big deal to some of you, but it has been huge for us.

Praying together on a regular basis was always something we wanted to do. We loved the idea of it! It sounded so spiritual and intimate. But, all of our attempts eventually ended in failure. After a few weeks we just ran out of gas for some reason.

After years of frustration we simply quit talking about it. We felt guilty when the topic came up in a sermon or book, because we knew we should be doing it.

Some of you are experiencing that feeling right now. Pretty awful, isn't it?

OK, I want you to cancel the guilt trip! It wasn't the guilt that made the difference for us. In fact, the guilt just made us feel more stressed, more stuck, and made me more irritable.

We started small. One day about a year-and-a-half ago I told Sandi, "I would like to start praying with you more often."

She said, "Sounds good."

That was it.

That night I reached for her hand after we got into bed and prayed a short, simple prayer.

The next night I did the same thing, and then the next...

After a few weeks Sandi instinctively began reaching for my hand after getting into bed. I am the one who prays most of the time. It was my suggestion and I assumed the responsibility for it. (There are some nights when I am too tired or discouraged to initiate prayer, and she always steps in.)

Why has prayer been such a big deal for us? It is a daily reminder that our Heavenly Father loves us and is with us.

One thing we have desperately needed on this journey has been courage. And prayer keeps our courage up. Praying together keeps us en–couraged (filled with courage).

As we pray we keep asking this question: "Where's the grace?"

By faith we visualize God going before us and making a way. Praying together helps us keep alert. We actively look for how God has gone before us and do our best to step into those situations, opportunities, and relationships that are somehow marked by God's grace.

A few examples:

- We made the decision to move to South Carolina after Sandi's boss unexpectedly agreed for her to work remote for ten months. That was a long shot in our minds, but this financial provision felt like God's grace to us.

- We decided to get involved at a certain church in town as we watched our daughter, Emily, begin making good friends and growing as a leader in the youth ministry. When Emily began referring to the church as "my church" we realized how much grace was already there.

- I have moved forward with the writing of this book due in large part to the constant encouragement and affirmation of Sandi. As others read the first chapter their positive feedback helps me to persevere. The grace I feel – that sense of God inviting me into something he is already doing – enables me to relax and keep writing.

But, by far the greatest evidence of God's grace that I now look for is unity with Sandi. As we talk about new opportunities, or try to make tough decisions, I want to know if we are in agreement. I want more than her ascent, I want to know we are on the same page in our minds and our hearts. Which means we need to talk a lot. It also means I have to be patient.

A recent example of this was an opportunity to get involved discipling students. I met with the youth pastor, appraised the situation, and was ready to jump in last May (four months ago). Sandi wasn't ready to give a heartfelt "yes" at the time. So, we agreed to host a student Bible study in our home for a month, and then re-assess the opportunity. We both felt encouraged by that experience, so we moved into more discussion with the youth pastor and our daughter (who was already serving in leadership). It made sense to both of us logically, but Sandi wanted to make sure it felt right relationally. So, we took our time and had several more conversations.

In the end we decided to serve. It was a six-month process that I wanted to complete in sixty minutes. By submitting to a process that Sandi felt more comfortable with, this decision became our decision. We both own it. I do not feel the pressure of dragging her into something she didn't want to do. And she doesn't feel the lack of respect or resentment that comes from feeling ran over.

We kept looking for the grace, and God kept giving us breadcrumbs.

Disclaimer: when looking for the grace you must hold the opportunity or relationship with an open hand. If you have already decided what you are going to do before praying and waiting on God to show you the way, then it's just a mockery. Let me tell you from personal experience, people know when they are being manipulated. Maybe not the first or second time, but they all catch on sooner or later.

In the end it all comes down to submission. Am I really willing to submit my agenda and compulsion for control to God's leadership? Will I wait or pass on the opportunity until I feel peace that God is inviting me into to? Will I refuse to damage the covenant relationship with my spouse by the way I am pursuing kingdom ministry?

So, for those of you who deeply care about making a difference in the world, please understand that God says, "It is not good" to be alone. We all need a helper suitable for us. God didn't bring Eve to Adam just because he was lonely and needed a mother for his children, God brought Eve because Adam could never accomplish all God had in mind for him alone. Marriage is covenant and kingdom. That's why marriage is a more complete reflection of God's glory.

A word to all of you who tend to sacrifice covenant for kingdom: If you want fruit that endures and a sustainable life and ministry, slow down, take stock, and invest strategically in your marriage. If you care about having a life worth imitating and becoming a leader worth following open the door and ask your spouse to come back in. Maybe it's not too late.

From Sandi

Tom asked if he could read chapter 6 out loud to me the day after he wrote it. We were sitting at the table eating lunch. He finished eating and pulled out his computer to read what he had written. It is always a vulnerable moment when you pour your heart out in writing and then read it to someone. He read the chapter and I listened. He has read other chapters and blogs to me out loud, but this one felt a bit different. By the time he got to the end of the chapter we both had tears in our eyes and I knew that God had done some healing in that very intimate moment. We both spoke words of confession and forgiveness and reveled in God's goodness and grace to us over the years. Tom's vulnerability and humility made me want to move toward him without fear. (Are you hearing this, guys?)

Our lunch date reinforced the things I wanted to write about in this chapter. When Tom was always running to the next exciting thing, I was dragging my heels and trying to slow him down. "Don't you see how wounded I am? Don't you know that we aren't ready to climb this mountain?" He kept pushing harder, and I felt guilty that I couldn't keep up or angry that he was leaving me behind. We pulled against each other and weren't making any progress. We had no vision or mission alignment. It was almost like a tug of war – he pulled one way, so for a long time I felt like I was supposed to pull the other way. This sinful cycle wasn't helping anything and I finally had to admit that my lack of boundaries was contributing to Tom's issues. OUCH!

I am a child of God and redemptive agent in this marriage. The world teaches us to repay evil for evil and good for good. Do to others as they do to you. Jesus teaches a different, better way that rises above fairness. So I had a difficult situation in my marriage. Tom was pulling away from me and I felt abandoned at times. I was tempted to distance myself from Tom as a way to get back at him or protect myself, and sometimes I did just that. If Tom was abandoning me for "the mission", it was not helpful for me to abandon him just to prove a point. It was helpful for me to say no to his abandonment and allow him to deal with his sin while I dealt with my own issues. It was also helpful for me to continue engaging when possible. If I want to show love and grace to anyone in the world, I first want to show it to my husband, especially when he is struggling. I knew clearly that Tom was struggling, so the most helpful thing I could do was submit my life to Christ, seek out my own healing (without holding Tom responsible for all of it) and get healthy myself so that I could come alongside and partner with him where possible.

Even though I had some bad days and struggled with wanting out of the pain, I was committed to being faithful. Pursuing my comfort and happiness is a shallow way to approach marriage. Faithfulness is what God clearly wanted for me, so I trusted that God would provide joy in His time.

I held onto hope and celebrated when Tom did engage and listen to me. Whenever he showed humility and vulnerability, I welcomed it and moved closer to him. I was careful not to "make him pay" for the hurt I was feeling. Instead I allowed him to see the impact his hurtful decisions were making on the family, but I remained open to reuniting whenever possible. I gave him grace and forgiveness knowing that God was going to meet my needs.

If you find yourself in what feels like a one-sided relationship, don't give up hope. Stay focused and keep doing what you know is right for the relationship. When your spouse shows any sign of humility or vulnerability, don't attack him or her! Make sure to reinforce that moment of intimacy by understanding that he or she is taking steps toward reconciliation. Treat their humility as a treasure and do not be condescending in any way. I have heard so many women say emasculating or demeaning things to their husbands when they are trying to apologize. "I'm sorry I hurt you" gets a response like, "Of course you hurt me and you should have known better, shame on you". This ugly response makes them feel like a child without respect. Be careful with these types of responses because it will make him or her NEVER want to apologize again. Move toward your spouse and respect their vulnerability. Make it a positive experience so they will want to continue to move toward you.

Rise above, be strong, be generous, be thankful, and God will give you grace that makes you a beautiful and desirable wife. Give it time and allow God to work. Repent of your mistakes and keep moving forward. Being a woman of God is your best plan to bring redemption into your marriage.

"People who always want to be happy and pursue it above all else are some of the most miserable people in the world. The reason is that happiness is a result. It is sometimes the result of having good things happen. But usually it is the result of our being in a good place inside ourselves and our having done the character work we need to do so that we are content and joyful in whatever circumstance we find ourselves. Happiness is a fruit of a lot of hard work in relationships, career, spiritual growth, or a host of other areas of life. But nowhere is this as true as in marriage." (Cloud and Townsend, *Boundaries in Marriage*, p. 109)

Chapter 7
From Isolation to Integration

The LORD God said, "It is not good for the man to be alone. I will make a helper suitable for him."... So the LORD God caused the man to fall into a deep sleep; and while he was sleeping, he took one of the man's ribs and then closed up the place with flesh. Then the LORD God made a woman from the rib he had taken out of the man, and he brought her to the man.

The man said, "This is now bone of my bones and flesh of my flesh; she shall be called 'woman,' for she was taken out of man."

That is why a man leaves his father and mother and is united to his wife, and they become one flesh.

Adam and his wife were both naked, and they felt no shame.

~ Genesis 2:18–25

The Genesis account of the first man, first woman, and first couple is a fascinating study of God's DNA for marriage. Through these twenty-five verses in the second chapter of Genesis we gain essential insights into God's original motivation for marriage.

So, before we go any further into what it looks like to have a marriage on mission, let's first align our basic understanding of marriage back to the factory settings. (When all else fails, read the manual!)

1. Before his introduction to Eve, Adam learned that love must be given freely

In the middle of the garden were the tree of life and the tree of the knowledge of good and evil. ~ Genesis 2:9

Before God creates the first marriage he teaches Adam something very important about the nature of love. How does he do this? By placing the tree of the knowledge of good and evil smack dab in the middle of his back yard and then telling him not to eat from it.

Now, why would God do that? I thought Eden was supposed to be perfect? What possible reason did God have for placing temptation within arm's reach of Adam and Eve? No tree, no temptation! No temptation, no sin!

Yes, God could have created Eden without the tree of the knowledge of good and evil. God could have made it impossible for Adam and Eve to sin. For that matter, God could have created robots that continually shout, "Praise God! Hallelujah!" twenty-four hours a day while bowing down and giving both their tithes and their offerings!

But that's not what God wanted. Perfect obedience was not his highest goal. God wanted something more; he wanted chosen obedience. God wanted Adam and Eve to love him freely, not because they had to, but because they chose to.

There is a word in the English language for forced love. That word is rape. God does not force his love.

God gave humanity the freedom to choose Him, or to choose something or someone else to love. That's why there had to be that tree. God values love given freely so much, that he was willing to risk it all.

Adam and Eve chose to love and walk with God. In the same way, they chose to love and walk with one another. Then, the day came they chose otherwise, and their relationship with God died. Soon after, the relationships with people began dying as well. It would take the birth, death and resurrection of the Second Adam to bring new life into those dead relationships; thus the price God paid to protect freedom.

2. Adam first experienced loneliness before God gave him companionship

Then the LORD God said, "It is not good for the man to be alone. I will make a helper suitable for him." ~ Genesis 2:18

If God knew that it wasn't good for man to be alone, why did he create Adam first? Why not create Adam and Eve at the same time? Why did God wait? Why was Adam asked to name all of the animals (I imagine them walking before him in pairs, male and female, snuggling and holding paws...) by himself?

Was this some kind of cruel joke? Is God playing mind games?

No, to the contrary, God loved Adam. God worked and sacrificed for Adam's greatest good. By making Adam wait for provision in the person of Eve, God actively loved Adam. God is love.

In wisdom God allowed Adam to experience what life was like without the companionship of an equal. He understood God's greatness and his own position as a created being. He understood his relationship and role among the animals and plants (to cultivate the garden and exercise his God-given authority). But there was no one standing by his side. No one uniquely designed for relationship with him. No hope for intimacy.

Not until God caused Adam to fall into a deep sleep, removed one of his ribs, and created Eve. I love Matthew Henry's quote on this:

> *"The woman was made of a rib out of the side of Adam;*
> *not made out of his head to rule over him, nor out of his*
> *feet to be trampled upon by him, but out of his side to be*
> *equal with him, under his arm to be protected, and near*
> *his heart to be beloved."*[3]

Isn't that beautiful? How would my life and marriage be different if every day I looked at Sandi as my equal who God has given me to protect and love?

I think God allowed Adam to go it alone for a time so that he could better appreciate the exquisitely crafted treasure he had in Eve. She was God's gift to Adam, and she was not to be taken for granted.

---

[3] Henry, Matthew. *Matthew Henry's Commentary on the Whole Bible: Complete and Unabridged in One Volume*, (Peabody, NY: Hendricksen, 1996).

3. Adam needed a "suitable helper"; he was not self-sufficient

In the same passage God says, *"I will make a helper suitable for him."* So, we surmise that Adam needed help, but with what?

Was he falling behind on his daily quota of animal naming? Were the tomatoes getting over-ripe? Were the elephants losing weight? Just what was it Adam needed Eve to help him with?

Three things stand out:

1. Since Adam was created in God's image, and since God lives in perfect communion through the relationships among the Trinity, Adam needed Eve to experience community. The zebras and weasels just weren't going to cut it! Adam needed someone who was like him, created as his equal, and designed to multiply God's glory with him.

2. Adam needed Eve to express and reflect the image of God. Genesis 1:27 says, *"So God created mankind in his own image, in the image of God he created them; male and female he created them."* God's image (and therefore, his glory) cannot be fully reflected in male or female, but only in male and female. You don't have to be married to reflect God's image, but none of us do it well alone.

3. Adam needed Eve to have children and co-parent a family. God commanded them to *"Be fruitful and increase in number."* Adam and Eve would subdue

and reign over all creation through their children's children. God's glory would be multiplied and his will accomplished on earth as it is in heaven through the ever-expanding human family. God's plan was to accomplish this through one man and one woman submitting to one another in the covenant of marriage. (And, that plan has yet to be improved upon.)

4. The marriage relationship is exclusive and takes precedence over all other human relationships

We read earlier that a man leaves his father and mother and unites with his wife. This "leaving" is an essential component of the marriage covenant. Ancient Jewish culture practiced the tradition of a man physically moving out of his parent's home into the new home that he and his bride would reside in (usually an addition built onto her parent's household). This was certainly a literal leaving, and is not to be overlooked. (Implication? If you are living with your wife in your parent's basement do everything in your power to get a decent job and move into your own place next week!)

The principle we see here speaks to the priority and exclusivity of marriage. No one is to compete with our affection and loyalty to one another, not even our parents. Hold on, are you ready for this? Not even our children (Gasp!). No one is to come between a husband and wife and invade that private and sacred space set-aside solely for the two of them. And this goes way beyond installing a good lock on your bedroom door (which you certainly should do). This touches upon hobbies (any hard core sports fanatics out there?). This includes other friendships (is your spouse confident you would choose him or her first to spend time with?). And don't forget your amusements that can turn into addictions. (How many hours did you spend shopping, on-line, or imbibing last week?)

5. Marriage is a full contact sport; a healthy sexual relationship is essential

This is not a book on sex, but we can't talk about a healthy marriage without talking about sex. So, let me just point out something and let you think it over: God's design for marriage is that two people become "one flesh". Not "one spirit"; not "one heart"; not "one mind"... There is no getting around it – sex is an integral, sanctified, and blessed aspect of marriage. God made procreation enjoyable. Amazing! And God also gave us sex for pleasure and bonding even when we are not procreating. Even more amazing!

In fact, the Bible permits married couples to abstain from sex only for short periods of time for the purpose of prayer and fasting (1 Corinthians 7:5). Then, they are instructed to resume their sexual relationship with a warning that if they don't they may lose self-control and get tempted by Satan. How many porn addictions and affairs could be prevented by consistently filling up one another's love tanks?

Here is an insight we have found extremely helpful: For Sandi, sex is connected to every other part of our relationship. If we are struggling in any area and have sex without first trying to resolve that issue, she feels used. On the other hand, sex makes me feel better connected with Sandi emotionally – thus more confident and secure in all other relationships. See the pattern? Emotional intimacy stirs the desire for sex in Sandi. Physical intimacy stirs the desire for emotional engagement within me. Isn't God a genius?

6. Christian marriage brings full disclosure without any shame

How many people know your secrets? How many people know your greatest failings and most embarrassing blunders? How many people know your darkest sins?

Adam and his wife were both naked, and they felt no shame.

~Genesis 2:25

Do you know what it feels like to stand in front of someone you love and trust completely naked without feeling an ounce of shame? We're not just talking about stripping down to your wedding rings before jumping into bed for a little sheet dancing; we are talking about complete transparency.

I find it interesting that James 5:16 says:

> *Confess your sins to each other and pray for each other so that you may be healed. The prayer of a righteous person is powerful and effective.*

What is the apparent correlation between confessing my sins to a brother or sister in Christ and getting healed? My hunch (and my experience) suggests that as I confess my sins to another person I bring my whole self into view – even those parts of me that bring shame and guilt. When I receive grace and my brother or sister prays for me, I find healing and release. My soul is reminded that God loved me while I was

115

still a sinner, powerless to please or obey him. Through this interaction I hear the words afresh, "you are my son, whom I love, with you I am well pleased..."

When Sandi loves me and prays for me despite my sins and failings, I find healing and new vision for a changed future. Those temptations and addictions begin to lose their power over me as they are brought into the light of Christian community. And it is then that I can stand before her, naked without shame.

Remember, you are only as sick as your secrets, especially in marriage.

And so, picking up our story, we were living in South Carolina and had just come through a bumpy first year. We both worked for 3DM for the first nine months of 2014, but due to a massive reorganization that shut down their central office in Pawleys Island, we were both let go (along with about 15 other people).

This was a difficult time for both of us, but a devastating blow for Sandi. She had quit her full time job in technology sales and taken a huge pay cut to work for 3DM. We worked together in the same office. Talk about moving from isolation to integration, we were practically attached at the hip! For a season it felt like this was why we had moved.

But this was not God's plan. In hindsight we now understand that our jobs with 3DM were bridges to something else God had for us, something still hidden at that time.

Sandi went back to technology sales with a new company. I ramped up my work coaching leaders and began investing more time with the Missionary Church again. For Sandi, these were painful setbacks. She was in mourning; the dream had died, again. She was angry with God. We ventured into the wilderness and ran around in circles for over a year, but now we were back in Egypt. We were in the exact same situation vocationally that we left behind in Michigan.

It felt like nothing had really changed. But, was this true?

On closer inspection something had changed; we had a taste of an integrated marriage and now had an appetite for it. And I was not willing to let it go. I was not willing to sit idly by and watch us slip back into the same ruts we left behind up north. As Sandi once again was becoming more absorbed in her work, more stressed, and less available to partner with me I spoke up. I took the initiative. I led.

I told her, "I feel like I am losing you again. I feel like we are losing us again. I don't believe God led us to move 850 miles so that you could work 50 hours a week in a job that consumes all of your time and drains all of your energy. I want my wife back. Will you quit this job and look for something part time? Will you join me in believing God for provision? Will you trust me to lead and take responsibility for our family's finances? Will you follow me into whatever God has in mind for us to do together?"

Which brings us full circle to this question: I can't do what God has asked me to do by myself. I need your help. Will you help me?

Don't miss this! Her "yes" to that question meant a "no" to her full time job and the security it afforded. (Every "yes" is a "no" to something when you think about it.)

In full possession of her "no" Sandi said "yes". So, the decision was made. Sandi would quit her full time job and find part time work that gave her the needed flexibility and margin for greater engagement with me. But when? Two weeks? Two months? Two years? We didn't know.

I did the only thing I knew to do; I asked a group of friends to pray for us.

Specifically I asked for two things:

1. Pray for God to transition Sandi into a part time job soon

2. Pray for God to give Sandi a time of rest – a sabbatical

A few days later I got an odd email from one of the pastors I asked to pray. He simply asked me, "How much money does Sandi make per month?"

I shot back the answer and pondered what was behind that question. I found out two days later when he asked this follow up: "If our church covers a month of her salary, will Sandi quit her full-time job, and take a one month sabbatical before starting a new part-time job?"

Are you kidding me? Who does this? We had never experienced sacrificial giving for the purpose of rest. What an amazing grace-gift we were being offered! Especially when you consider that we never asked for money – just for God's timing and provision. Was this God's answer? Should Sandi quit her job immediately and rest for a month before going back to work part time?

This was an easy decision for her. Yes, God was obviously answering our prayer! Yes, she would quit her job and take a month off to rest. Yes, we would trust God for the right part time job. And yes, we would also trust God for the sizable gap this would create in our family budget, yet again.

But more importantly, we were both willing to re-enter the wilderness. Going back to Egypt just wasn't an acceptable option. No matter how long it took or how much it cost, we were going to see this through. We were both fully invested, totally committed. For better or worse...

Keep in mind that when you enter the wilderness, like Israel did under the leadership of Moses, you walk through three stages. Walter Brueggeman writes about the following progression in *Praying the Psalms*:

1. Orientation

2. Dis-orientation

3. Re-orientation

You begin with the known and familiar (orientation). Dictionary.com defines orientation as: "the ability to locate oneself in one's environment with reference to time, place, and people".

Orientation is normal, stable life. It is the real world of our daily experience. It's not perfection, but it is known and feels safe. When we feel oriented our lives make sense to us. (The Jews became oriented in Egypt as slaves. The reality of their situation was exploitation and suffering, but they accepted their circumstances as the norm.)

And, that's the danger; no matter how bad your situation you can get accustomed to it over time. Thousands of couples just accept the sad reality of their broken dreams and marriages. Fear and hopelessness hold them fast, and they eventually look for intimacy and impact elsewhere. Or, they just quit looking all together and find ways to numb the pain.

Sandi and I reached a place where we quit looking for answers. Our relationship had devolved into chaos and stress when you peered just beneath the surface. We felt helpless, frustrated, and utterly stuck. We had crossed over into dis-orientation.

Dis-orientation brings stress, conflict, and assaults our faith. Confusion reigns. Often marriages end right here. Dis-orientation is entering the wilderness of the unknown and unfamiliar. We feel turned upside down and inside out; our long held assumptions buckle.

But for some couples a moment comes when they say "no more!" They reach a place of honesty and brokenness that leads them back to the message of Jesus: *"Repent and believe the good news."* (Mark 1:15) Repentance involves owning our mistakes and wrongs and turning away from a self-centered, self-directed, and self-reliant lifestyle. Believing the good news involves placing our trust in the person and work of Jesus and choosing to love and follow him as our first priority. (This isn't just about fixing your marriage; it goes far deeper.)

Couples that are willing to take a very sobering look into the mirror and begin addressing the real issues enter stage three: Re-orientation.

Breaking through the frustration and despair of disorientation is a giant step forward. With renewed hope we begin our journey into re-orientation. We are making changes! We are getting help! We are talking about issues that were swept under the rug years ago. We are finally making progress. It's a brand new day.

But there is still a long journey ahead. Soon we begin to wilt under that hot sun as we realize there is more desert to cross. Water is hard to come by and we start having second thoughts. As buried issues begin to resurface we wonder if we would have been better off back in Egypt. This part of the journey is much harder than we expected. What "should" have taken a few weeks drags on for months. We learn the hard way that re-orientation is a process that involves a lot of effort. It becomes a daily waiting upon God as our only source of hope and strength.

To enter the Promised Land we must be willing to embrace the whole Gospel message; we die with Jesus on the cross, we are buried with Jesus, and we rise to new life with Jesus (Romans 6). Re-orientation is resurrection, not self-help. Re-orientation is empowered by the Spirit of God, not by our best efforts.

So, Sandi walked away from a good job with benefits to join me on a desert journey. We embarked on this leg of the race less than three months ago at the time of this writing. We've had many good days and a few really bad ones. God has already opened doors for partnership and impact that we couldn't bring ourselves to hope for a few years ago. And thus far he has sustained us financially and emotionally. We have been reminded of an old truth: his mercy is new every morning. When our provisions run out, his manna falls from the sky to meet each need, at times in rather dramatic fashion.

As we walk toward what God has prepared for us we are learning how to walk together. We are learning a great deal about pacing. I am learning how to slow my sprint into a steady stride that makes room for life and relationships (and even fun). Sandi is learning to walk by faith into new arenas that remind her of past pain and isolation. She is stepping out with both courage and determination. And together we are finding our way...and each other.

From Sandi

Moving to South Carolina was not a quick and easy fix. My dream of walking hand in hand into the spiritual sunset of ministry partnership did not pan out as I hoped. Old fears crept in and I kept thinking of the story of Abraham and Sarah and the promise that God made to them about a child. It wasn't happening fast enough so they took matters into their own hands. Sarah gave her servant Hagar to Abraham, thinking maybe that would speed things up. Most sermons I hear on this Old Testament story focus on Sarah and Abraham and how they should have faith to trust God. This time I thought about Hagar and how she was NOT the mother of the promised, blessed child. She did her part but the promise was not meant for her and she needed to flee. That story scared me, terrified me actually because I wondered if my situation was similar. Did I misunderstand God's promise? Am I Sarah or Hagar in this story? Is God's promise meant for me or am I on the sidelines watching other people live out the promises of God?

So when my ministry job ended in SC, I immediately went back to doing what I knew how to do and found a technology sales job in the area. I once again began to mourn the loss of my ministry dream. I was thankful for finding a job so quickly and God used it to help provide as Tom made some personal ministry transitions. But God did not want me to stay in technology sales and I knew it after only a few months. I started falling back into some old habits, blaming my schedule and feeling like a victim. I once again needed to take ownership of my stress level and make whatever changes were necessary to engage with life and ministry in a meaningful way. Tom and I started to pray for breakthrough.

We started asking a few people to join us in praying for my job and stress, and God provided in an amazing way. A pastor and friend called Tom and offered to send support money if I would quit my job, take a month off, and find a part time job instead. I had already decided that I really needed to quit my job and help Tom with this book and focus on our ministry, but I just didn't know when I should do it. This financial gift (which was about a month's income) turned out to be just the encouragement I needed to quit right away and hope again in God's promises. It gave me a month sabbatical to rest and heal. What an amazing blessing! God is faithful and I am learning that his promises are true and he has not cast me aside or put me on a shelf!

Without death there can be no resurrection.

I did find a part time office job almost immediately after my sabbatical. But just yesterday I found out that business is slow and they won't need me anymore. I texted Tom and told him that my part time job was over, to which he replied, "good...I think". Trusting God with this is certainly a daily commitment. To be honest I'm a bit discouraged about it today. It seems like I should be getting used to this idea, but it is still always a struggle. I'm not panicked right now, just uneasy. Today (and tomorrow and the next day)

I will have to give God my fears and trust that He will provide.

God has some work to do in me and my identity in Christ. I have to learn that my identity in Christ is based on God's love for me. I am not a Christian because I obey and do good works for the Father. I am a Christian because the Father has a love relationship with me through Jesus Christ that empowers me to obey and do good works. That perspective changes everything for me as I receive God's power instead of working to earn God's acceptance. I am a child of the King! Regardless of my job, my ministry, my place of employment, or my state of residence, I am God's child and can have confidence in who I am. It takes losing these things (some of them multiple times) for me to learn that.

Chapter 8
New Patterns of Missional Faithfulness

"Being deeply loved by someone gives you strength, while loving someone deeply gives you courage."
– Lao Tzu

"Love must be as much a light, as it is a flame."
– Henry David Thoreau

After the big move to South Carolina in 2013 Sandi and I were faced with the question of what we intended to do with this fresh start God had given us. The only thing we knew for certain was we didn't want to slip back into old patterns of compartmentalization, isolation, and self-centeredness. We hungered for integration and mission. We actually believed the whole "go far together" stuff, but we didn't know where to start.

A few weeks after unpacking boxes we heard Mike Breen speak on this topic. In fact, the title of his talk was, "Family on Mission". Bringing the ideas of family and mission together was exactly what we were trying to do. It had to be both covenant and kingdom, both relationship and responsibility.

We were ready for this!

The gist of the training?

1. Jesus lived his life UP, IN, and OUT

2. As followers of Jesus we also live our lives UP, IN, and OUT

3. We start small, and aim for simple and sustainable

The 3-Dimensional Life of Jesus

A quick survey of the Gospels demonstrates the simple and powerful pattern of Jesus' life; he lived upwards toward his Father, inwards toward his followers, and outwards toward a lost world.

Take Mark 1 for instance. After his baptism and testing in the wilderness (which both demonstrated his love and fidelity to his Father – his upward relationship) he called his first disciples. In verse 17 he called Peter and Andrew to follow him as apprentices (IN). *"Come, follow me," Jesus said, "and I will send you out to fish for people."* Notice Jesus weds the vision of fishing for people (OUT) to the invitation to follow (IN).

He then goes to Capernaum and sets a man free by driving out an impure spirit (OUT). The next stop is Peter's home where he heals Peter's mother-in-law (IN) and then works late into the night healing the sick and freeing the demonically oppressed as the entire town gathers at the house (OUT and IN). What does Jesus do after such an exhausting night meeting so many needs? He wakes up before sunrise to spend time alone with his Father (UP).

And, so it goes.

We see the same when examining Jesus' teaching. In Matthew 22 he is asked to identify the greatest commandment in the Law. To which he replied:

> *"Love the Lord your God with all your heart, and all your soul, and all your mind. This is the greatest commandment. And the second is like it: Love your neighbor as yourself. All the Law and the Prophets hang on these two commandments."*

In his summary of what was most important in the revealed word of God Jesus basically said, "Love God (UP) and love people (IN and OUT)."

OK, this seems pretty obvious, right? Jesus lived a 3-dimensional life and trained his followers to do the same. As his disciples (learners) they did what they saw him doing and spoke what they heard him saying. As the consummate show-and-tell leader Jesus modeled and taught his followers how to replicate his 3-dimensional life. Which is exactly what we see them doing in the book of Acts.

Sandi and I were convinced! But where to start? We felt overwhelmed...

Until we heard this simple suggestion: "since most of you eat every day, set aside one meal a week for UP, one for IN, and one for OUT".

Could it be that simple? You mean to say that we can take three meals out of the twenty-one we eat every week and repurpose them for UP, IN, and OUT? C'mon, there has to be more to it!

Well, of course there's more to it, but this was an excellent place to start. It was certainly a small step, it was simple, and it didn't feel too heavy for us, so we thought it might be sustainable. And, I am happy to say two years later we are going stronger than ever!

Here's what we did:

- Tuesday night dinner became our UP night. We told the kids not to make any plans, sat together as a family, ate a good meal, read a chapter of the Bible, discussed it, and then prayed for one another. That's it. No preparation required, just a Bible and someone to keep track of the chapter we read last week.

- Thursday night dinner became our IN night. Again, we made this a priority in our family calendar and avoided other commitments. We simply invited a Christian family over for dinner, had a good time getting to know them, talked about our "highs and lows" for the week, and if there was an obvious need prayed for one another.

- For OUT Sandi and I repurposed our walks through the neighborhood (something we were already doing) into prayer walks. We went out of our way to be friendly to everyone we met and worked hard to learn names. We prayed for several people on the spot as concerns surfaced. Then, we began inviting these folks back into our home for a monthly brunch. We flip pancakes, ask a few people to bring a dish to pass, and make lots of coffee. We usually have 10 – 15 people in our home for these brunches, and the only agenda is blessing our neighbors and building relationships. We pray that God will direct us to those people he is already drawing to himself, and then we follow up with them. Again, pretty simple.

Just this afternoon Sandi took our dog, Rocky, for a walk. She met two new neighbors and talked with others who had already joined us for a brunch. As we meet new people we simply say, "Hey, we are kind of new around here and are trying to get to know our neighbors. We have a few people over about once a month for brunch, would you like to join us next time?"

Then, the next time we see them on a walk we give them the date (we have scheduled the next brunch for October 31, two weeks from now). Sometimes we print up simple invitations with our address and cell numbers on them, sometimes its just word of mouth. We keep it casual and low pressure. If they don't come this month we know there will be another one soon enough. We pray that God will bring exactly who he wants each time, and really don't worry too much about it. Once only a few people showed up and we had a great time getting to know them in a more intimate setting!

Here are the top ten things we have learned along the way:

1. Establish these patterns and stay focused on them, but give yourself grace. There will be weeks when one of the kids is sick, when you have to travel for work, or when you are just too busy with other things that popped up. Don't sweat it! Our goal is to hit 3 out of 4

times. So, if we hit 75% we feel great about it. If we dip to 50% or lower we make adjustments.

2. Be flexible, but stay stubborn. Tomorrow night is Tuesday but we are having a family from church over for dinner (normally that would be an IN focus for us, which should happen on Thursday night). So, we will do our UP as a family on Thursday this week. We are able to interchange Tuesday and Thursday nights, but so far have been unsuccessful switching to another night of the week.

3. Be creative. I have joined our family for UP on speakerphone, and we have Skyped our oldest daughter into family meals. These are not ideal, but some connection is better than no connection.

4. There are certain seasons of the year that just don't work well – like Christmas vacation, major holidays, and certain weeks during the summer. Rest up during these periods and come back strong next time. Remember, 3 out of 4 on average is the goal. (Also, be open to experimenting with something new. Try mixing it up from time to time when the normal rhythm is not workable.)

5. For our UP nights, I read a chapter of the Bible and then, without commentary, pass the Bible around the table. Each person talks about what stood out to them and why. Resist the temptation to preach a sermon! Keep your input brief, personal, and sincere. When

possible, ask everyone to share a prayer request and to pray for someone else.

6. Prayer walking our neighborhood consistently is the key for us. We walk 3 or 4 days a week, sometimes more often (living in South Carolina helps!). Our secret? Smile, talk with those who smile back, and invite them to the next brunch if they seem open. Also, be sure to clean up your dog's poo from their lawn – we want to be good news as we earn the opportunity to share the Good News. Seriously.

7. Look for other Christ followers in your neighborhood and ask them to join you. We are developing friendships with a few Christian families and I have asked some to partner with us. So far that just means come when you can, pray for your neighbors, and invite someone new to our next brunch.

8. Be very discerning about inviting people to church. We live in the south, so just about everybody will tell you they belong to this or that church. Some of them are faithfully worshipping and serving, others are not. Either way, if a church invitation comes too quickly your brunch (or whatever you do) can quickly turn into a recruiting conversation that turns people off. Focus on building a friendship first. Once you get to know each other better and they see your heart for God conversations about church naturally arise. Be patient, no one wants to feel like your project.

9. Set the dates for your OUTs early. Whatever you decide to do get it in the calendar so that you can talk to people about it and extend invitations. The old, "Let's get together for dinner sometime" usually means, "I want you to like me and believe I care about you, but I am honestly too busy to invest time into a relationship with you". That may sound harsh, but let's call it what it is.

10. Pay special attention when people are under tension or experiencing transition. We recently brought a meal to our neighbors after a death in the family. A few months back we prayed for a man facing an amputation. This past year we have cut the grass for an older couple grappling with cancer. And just yesterday I mailed a card to the man who manages the restaurant our son works at who is recovering from neck surgery. These little touches mean so much to people under tension. Also, pay attention to new people moving into the neighborhood. A plate of cookies to a new neighbor can be the most spiritual thing you do all week!

How to follow up with responsive people

OK, so we are having literally dozens of people into our home just about every month. What are you supposed to do with them?

Here is a practical strategy derived from the way Jesus first called disciples and his teaching on the *"person of peace"* in Luke 9 and 10.

1. It all starts with friendship

Whether the relationship is IN or OUT, it all starts with knocking on the door of friendship. (Remember, Jesus was called a "friend of sinners".) A friendship happens when two or more people spend time together, care about some of the same things, feel a certain connection with one another, and like being together.

I say we knock on the door of friendship because you can't force it. If you find someone you believe may develop into a friend you knock, but only they can open that door (and even then, only God's grace can pull you together).

Some ways to knock?

- Learn their name and call them by it the next time you see them. This indicates you paid attention and care about them. I must confess to cheating with this! Within 30 seconds after walking away from someone I meet for the first time I have my phone out and am writing down their name and something about them to help me remember who they are. I have a category in my contacts called POP (People of Peace) where I record this. We have lived in our neighborhood for just over one year and I have eighty-eight names recorded. Next to some names I include the name or breed of their dog, or the name of the neighbor they live next to, or how we prayed for them. I can't emphasize this enough! We believe that God loves each of them and knows them by name, shouldn't we help to communicate that truth?

- Invite them into a connecting opportunity (like our brunches) and see who responds. The response rate for our brunches has probably been about 30%. We don't get offended by those who don't come; we just keep smiling and talking to them whenever we get the chance. But, we pay special attention to those who do respond and choose to spend time with us.

- Don't overlook the little things. Help with their dog when they are out of town. (Are you picking up the whole dog theme? Getting a puppy four months ago has sparked scores of conversations.) Share your cherry tomatoes when the garden produces too many. Pick up trash from their yard as you walk by. Stop and talk when the opportunity arises, even if it wasn't on your agenda. Follow up on prayer requests to see how God is answering. And be a good neighbor by cutting your grass, keeping your pets under control, and waving hello to people when you pass them on the road. Little acts of kindness and respect over time can warm hearts and unlock doors.

- Invite them to lunch or coffee. This Thursday I am having lunch with a young man who just moved into our neighborhood a few months ago. He is certainly in transition and my guess is that he is also feeling the tension of loneliness. We will talk about hunting and fishing and chances are good we will spend more time together this fall. My gut tells me this is an OUT relationship and right now I sense that God is already at work. Tomorrow I will eat lunch with another man who I believe God wants me to partner with to bless our neighborhood somehow. He has been a person of peace to me and has already connected me with several new people.

- Focus your time and energy on the responsive. Don't give up on those who shy away, but make yourself more available to those who smile back and are open to friendship.

2. Some friends turn into followers

The key question here becomes; "We are following Jesus, would you like to join us?" Again, this applies to both IN and OUT relationships. We are basically asking people to sojourn with us on our journey toward modeling, making, and multiplying missionary disciples. It doesn't matter where they begin this journey, the focus becomes their next step and which direction it takes them. For those who don't know Christ yet the starting point is entering a relationship with him and experiencing a spiritual re-birth. For those already in a relationship with Jesus the conversation often centers on how they are modeling the life of Jesus (do they have a life worth imitating yet?). Information without an imitatable life is not only ineffective; it is counter-productive and can be dangerous.

Indications that friends want to become followers?

- Who seems interested in spiritual conversations? When you ask a good question that opens the God topic, are they willing to go there? When you share a recent example from your life about how God is blessing or growing your faith, do they listen with interest? These sorts of conversations can happen at any moment with anybody. We are not talking about a Bible study or inviting people to church. This is life on life. This is about you loving your neighbor as you love yourself.

- Pay attention to who sticks around to help with the dishes or pick up the living room. I especially look for this early on with IN relationships. I am far less impressed by the aspiring theologian who wants to teach next time than I am by the young person who stays an extra fifteen minutes and helps out. The people of peace in Luke 9 and 10 opened their homes, shared meals, and opened up networks. Covenant faithfulness precedes kingdom fruitfulness – so look for people willing to serve in a relational way.

- Co-followers are ready and willing to serve right now. Remember, they are not serving us (in a selfish sense); they are serving God and the mission he sent us on. In youth ministry we always talked about FAT people: Faithful, Available, and Teachable. In other words, these people develop into servants, leaders, and givers, not simply consumers.

- When the time is right, ask someone to step up and take on responsibility. Could we meet in their home next month? Will they bring a salad? Will they pray for our group? Will they follow up next week with this or that? Will they introduce us to their friends?

- Look for grace in kind. For example, Sandi and I have been invited over for dinner by two neighbors. These are both IN relationships, and you better believe we are paying close attention to these families. This is the kind of grace we look for! (Keep those ratios in mind. We have personally met about one hundred people, we've had about sixty in our home, and only two families have reciprocated. This is a slow process and if you are thin-skinned it's going to be extremely difficult.)

3. Some followers want to join your family

Here's how this has worked for us. You meet eighty-eight people over the course of a year, and a handful of them (maybe a dozen in our case) become friends. These are not deep relationships yet, but good seed has encountered good soil and good things are growing. Out of those twelve people, four of them begin following Christ at your side. They are following you also – as you follow Christ (1 Corinthians 11:1). You are serving Christ together as friends and co-laborers and they are imitating your life. You are in the same boat pulling on the oars and heading in the same direction.

The next step? A couple of those followers become family. The difference? Family members sacrifice for one another, and spiritual families have stronger allegiances to those doing God's will than to they do to their own relatives (including parents, children, and siblings).

Jesus modeled this for us. In Mark 3 his family travels to where he is teaching and healing vast crowds of people planning to *"take charge of him"* because they believed he was *"out of his mind."* They arrived at the house where Jesus and his disciples were staying, but because of the press of people can't get to him. So, they sent a message, and soon someone told Jesus, *"Your mother and brothers are outside looking for you."*

Jesus responded to their request in a manner that must have shocked everyone in the room and deeply offended his family. Looking at his disciples sitting with him he said, *"Here are my mother and my brothers! Whoever does God's will is my brother and sister and mother."*

Can you feel the tension?

Jesus made it perfectly clear that his top priority was to do God's will (UP, IN, and OUT) and align himself with others who did likewise. These disciples became his spiritual family, and those bonds went deeper than flesh and blood.

Has God given you a spiritual family? If so, how do you recognize them?

Here are a few characteristics:

- Spiritual family members come to you through the channels of friendship and followership. They do not appear out of thin air.

- As you become more faithful and fruitful in your own relationship with God, potential spiritual family members gravitate towards you. The implication? If you are lukewarm in the way you are following Jesus you will attract other lukewarm Christians. You may desire a spiritual family, but you will, in fact, send the signal that you are not a safe person they can trust yet.

- Spiritual families sacrifice for one another. In other words, they give until it hurts. They open their homes for extended periods of time. They give generously when there is a need (think of the early church in Acts selling property and giving the proceeds to the Apostles to care for the poor). They make time for each other, share meals together, serve together, and basically do life in community. In times of sorrow they weep with one another. In times of celebration they rejoice with one another.

- Because a spiritual family is a family on mission, their love for God and commitment to his mission trump all else. This means they speak the truth to one another, even when it's hard to hear.

- Spiritual families learn how to prune back the entanglements of this world to safeguard space in their lives for God, his mission, and each other. Often mature leaders will arise in a local context and function as spiritual parents guiding the family and modeling loyalty to Christ above all else.

The two best resources I know of for those who want to study this further are *Real Life Discipleship* by Jim Putman, and *Family on Mission* by Mike and Sally Breen. I recommend both books highly.

Another tool that has proven extremely helpful is the "Discipleship Funnel" Steve Jones created (the same mentor who shared "If you want to go fast, go alone. If you want to go far, go together" with me). This tool captures the process Jesus used to move people from friends all the way to family. I love visual tools, and this one is a keeper!

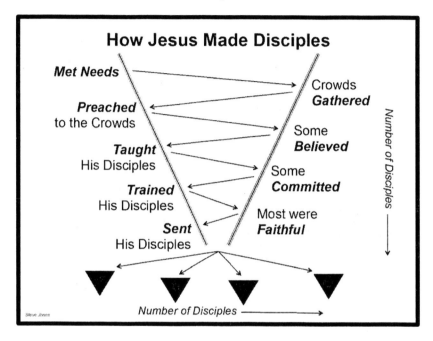

This illustrates the pattern so often observed in Christ's life:

1. Jesus encounters needy people and meets their needs. Jesus often first meets people at their point of need. The most common needs he met in the Gospels were physical healing, spiritual cleansing (driving out impure spirits), and most importantly filling empty souls by incarnating God's grace and truth by what he did and said. (On occasion, he even filled empty stomachs.) The principle? Jesus came full of grace and truth – but most often led with grace.

2. As Jesus met deep needs in miraculous fashion, word quickly spread and large crowds gathered. Some came genuinely seeking the Messiah, others to see the show, and a few to find fault in an imposter. But, for whatever the reason, they came in the thousands. How did Jesus respond? He preached the Good News of the Kingdom. He declared that the time had come to repent and believe in him as the promised One.

3. The reaction? Some believed, but most walked away. He was not the conquering Son of David they longed for. Many felt insulted, especially the religious. Why should they have to repent?

4. He taught those who believed. These were smaller settings, questions were asked, explanations given, and stories told. Old men were instructed on what it meant to be born again during late night tutorials. Tax collectors were enlightened on God's justice for those they robbed, but also on God's mercy for the humble sinner. Immoral women learned that Jesus did not come to condemn the world, and judgmental men learned to consider their own sin before condemning another. But most importantly, his followers found both grace and truth in not only his teachings, but also his way of life. They were literally becoming "little Christs" (the definition of word "Christian"). They were also known as "followers of the Way".

5. Those who committed themselves to not only listen to his teachings, but to actually do what he asked (a very small percentage) were trained. And those he trained,

he sent out to reproduce the entire process until the whole world was changed. (If you've never read Robert Coleman's classic, *The Master Plan of Evangelism* go to Amazon right now and order it! Trust me.)

And so, for the past two years Sandi and I have committed ourselves to the rhythms of UP, IN, and OUT. In many ways we are like a 3-year old learning how to ride a bike. We wobble along. Our training wheels safeguarding us from serious injury as our muscles strengthen and our balance improves. Revival has not broken out. The sick have not been healed nor the dead raised. Not yet.

But we are far from discouraged. We know if we continue to wobble along God will continue to shape our character and grow our competencies. Jesus spent three years investing primarily in twelve men, and they still had much growing to do after his ascension. What makes me think it should be any easier for us? Why would God's visible kingdom come in my neighborhood or church more quickly than what Jesus experienced? We are just getting started.

Tonight Sandi and I coach four or five ministry couples in the works, words and ways of Jesus. This Sunday we share our story and teach the methods of Jesus to a church in Michigan. Next month we host a retreat for ministry couples and share with them some of what God has poured into us. When God blesses you he always intends for that blessing to multiply. Our lives and marriage are becoming conduits of God's grace...isn't that the whole idea?

From Sandi

UP – IN – OUT patterns.

Tom does a great job describing how we as a family are serious about scheduling UP – IN – and OUT times in our family calendar. I talk to other women and I get mixed responses. Some think it is a good idea, but just never quite get around to doing it. The biggest obstacle seems to be busyness. Most parents work full time jobs, kids are involved in multiple sports and activities, and it can be overwhelming to add one more thing into an already crammed schedule. I remember sitting at the dinner table one night talking to Tom about a new ministry option and I literally held up my hands and said, "Do not ask me to do one more thing". I could not and would not add another thing to our calendar. So here's the rub; we want to do ministry, but we don't have time for it, so we feel guilty and wonder why we never see kingdom breakthrough in our lives.

A turning point for me happened at a conference where I heard a lady talking about her family schedule. She wrote out her family mission statement and then drew several circles on a whiteboard and labeled each one with a family activity or schedule requirement. Her list included things like: carpool to school, soccer practice, church, date night, meals, dance classes, small group, decorate the house.... She then worked to see how any of the circles supported or distracted from the mission statement and where they intersected with each other. She explained how she tried to eliminate any of the circles that stood alone. For example, she was looking at buying a new home and had her eye on a certain classy neighborhood. She realized that the neighborhood was farther away from the school, the church, and her established ministries. Even though she had the freedom to buy a house in any neighborhood, she knew that if she bought the house it would add a ten-minute drive to almost anywhere she had to go – that can really add up if you are trying to be strategic with your time! She also realized she was carpooling her kids over forty-five minutes each way so they could attend a certain school, and the school circle didn't intersect with any other circles, and most of the people at this school lived even farther away. While she loved eating out and trying new restaurants, she recognized that purposely going to a select few local places helped her start building relationships with people. You get the idea; she evaluated each circle based on how it served her mission and how it connected to other circles. Some things had to change. She had to simplify her life and make decisions based on how each activity fit into the whole. Maybe it's an honor for her son to play on the travel baseball team, but it is not best for her family mission, so she declines and lets her son play for the local rec team. We don't have to sign our kids up for every single opportunity and we are certainly not bad parents if we insist on some family time. Saying no to activities makes life simpler, but it is not easy to do.

Everything is a choice! If you want to implement rhythms of UP-IN-OUT then you will have to reorient your schedule to make it a priority. You have to model it and avoid getting sucked into a busy/reactive lifestyle. In our situation, we have two high school kids living at home and there are ALWAYS demands on the schedule. Emily and Grant are in school sports, clubs, have jobs, and are active in youth group. We picked Tuesday and Thursday as our nights and overall require that the kids do not schedule anything on those nights. Sometimes this is impossible (baseball tournament or band concert) but overall it is possible. This means that the kids are not available to work those nights, it means if someone asks us out to dinner on one of those nights we can honestly say we already have plans. It means if any of us want to join something new that meets on one of those nights we say no. It means we are intentional and sometimes it comes with a price, but we believe the benefits far outweigh the sacrifices. This rhythm is a priority and we treat it as such. The most difficult thing we said no to was when a youth group leader asked Emily if she could join a girls discipleship group on Tuesday nights. I struggled with this because I wanted Emily to be in a discipleship group, but I had to say no. There will always be things competing for our time and taking us away from our consistent rhythms. You have to choose wisely and be willing to eliminate some good things to focus on the best things. I honestly think my kids will be better off having experienced some healthy family rhythms that show them how to love God and others in a tangible way. Now there might be times when we switch to different nights and we have to make sure our rhythm serves the mission. Once the rhythm becomes legalistic then it is time to make adjustments and keep moving forward!

For us the monthly Saturday brunch works. The key here is to keep it simple. I don't clean the house for hours before each brunch. I don't scour the Internet for fantastic recipes that will show off my cooking skills. I purposely make it simple and repeatable. I show respect for my guests by removing the families' pile of shoes from the entryway and I make sure there are no dirty socks decorating the bathroom floor, but overall I don't fuss. Some women I know get very stressed about having people in their home. I had to come to grips with the fact that my desire to be perfect or show off a spotless home was my pride, and it didn't serve the value of building relationships or reaching out to neighbors. This is life-on-life ministry and the most spiritual thing I can do in this situation is to set aside my pride and let people into my life. You have to be comfortable with people seeing the real you, your real home, and your real strengths and weaknesses. Once people see that you are approachable and not perfect, the walls come down and they become more open to friendship.

This has been a slow and sometimes painful process. I'm still searching to find good friends to do life together and enjoy IN fellowship. I often feel disconnected with people in my neighborhood. I have to trust God that he will provide the right friends and the right ministry opportunities as I serve faithfully. Regardless of my season of life or the demands on my schedule, I have committed to the priorities of time with God, time with other Christians, and time reaching out to a lost world.

I have heard you can evaluate someone's priorities by looking at how they spend their money. I think it is equally true that you can determine someone's mission and values by looking at how they spend their time. Show me what you value most by how you spend your money and time. This is how you model, make, and multiply disciples.

Chapter 9
The Abrahamic Calling:
Signposts in the Distance

I begin writing this final chapter at the Hartsfield-Jackson International Airport in Atlanta, Georgia. I suppose it's fitting to write about our future path from the busiest airport on planet earth.

I have not slept in my own bed for seven nights, and I have not seen Sandi for six days. I am homesick and a little heartsick. Here's why...

Over the past week I have:

- Had coffee with a national non-profit rep who is actively raising funds to invest in the health of pastors and their marriages. His group is responding to the current relational crisis so many ministry couples find themselves in.

- Had dinner with a church planting couple I have coached the past two years who are starting missional communities in their apartment complex (they also have four kids under twelve and own a growing tech company). They are stretched incredibly thin and often knocked off balance.

- Met with a church planting couple who are mourning the death of their church plant and trying to figure out who they are now and if God still has a plan for their lives (mostly I wept with them – this all-too-familiar story is heart wrenching)

- Coached another pastor in a very successful church (by normal standards) who has a "ministry death wish". The pressure of "feeding the machine" is so intense and he feels so alone that he told me he would be relieved if the whole thing folded.

- Coached another church planter and network leader who is trying to hold together a marriage, young family, full time job as an executive in a growing company, and his own church plant while laying the foundation for a church planting network. He is walking a tight rope and we are keeping a very close eye on his health and his marriage (I invite his wife into half of our coaching calls to keep things honest). They are managing well right now – but how long can they withstand this pace and pressure? They are both rock stars in my book, but what does healthy covenant and sustainable kingdom ministry look like for them?

I don't share all of this to impress you with how busy I am, or what a good job I am doing for God. I share this because I want you to catch a glimpse of what I see almost every day; the life of the average ministry leader is fraught with struggle and besieged with ever increasing pressure. Some self-destruct, but most of these leaders love Jesus, remain faithful to their spouse and family, and want to make a difference for the Gospel. But too many are losing hope, too many are buckling under the pressure, and too many have hearts growing harder and colder the longer they serve as Christian leaders.

Something is broken.

Here's what the latest research from The Fuller Institute and George Barna tells us:

- 1500+ pastors left the profession each month last year

- Only 1 in 8 seminary graduates retire in vocational Christian ministry

- 80% of pastor's wives wish their husbands were engaged in other occupations

- 77% of pastors felt they did not have a good marriage

- 71% of pastors stated they were burned out, battling depression beyond fatigue on a weekly and even a daily basis

- 70% of pastors have no close personal friends, no one in whom to confide

The two statistics that tug most at my heart? 77% of pastors say they don't have a good marriage! (No wonder the vast majority of their spouses wish they had a regular job instead of "working for the Lord".) The other one? 70% of pastors say they have no close personal friends.

Give that a moment to settle.

Three quarters of our pastors are struggling in their marriages, some acutely. Most of those leading our churches feel like they are all alone...friendless.

What the hell is going on? (I don't use the term lightly.)

The reasons for the leadership crisis that exists today in the American church are many. I do not have the expertise to diagnose and suggest a treatment plan for 350,000 churches. Like the Samaritan woman in John 4 I simply have my own story to tell. And, like her, I am discovering just how universal my story truly is.

The sad reality is that at one time I was the poster child for 6 out of 6 of those depressing statistics I quoted above.

6 out of 6...

That means I:

- Left the ministry and had no plans to re-enter it

- Didn't feel like we had a good marriage

- Felt depressed and burned out

- Had a wife suggesting other career options

- Felt very alone – the only person I believed understood me was my counselor

The very fact that I am now in a healthy marriage and ministry is a tribute to God's grace. The reality that Sandi and I actually want to be married (to each other no less!) and choose to serve together is pretty incredible.

It is the hope embedded in our story that motivated you to read this book. And guess what? You have a story to tell also. And the next chapter of that story can begin today (yes, I know that sounds trite but it is absolutely true). Is today a turningpoint for you and your marriage? Is today the day you repent and believe the good news on behalf of your most important relationship?

What does the next chapter of our story look like? To be honest, God has not revealed that to us yet. Will we continue living in Pawleys Island after our youngest graduates high school? Will we someday serve on the staff of a local church again? Will I finally hit my growth spurt and reach 5'9" before I turn 50?

We simply do not know (except for that last one!).

We don't know yet because God has placed a certain kind of call on our lives. We are experiencing an Abrahamic calling, not a Mosaic calling.

What's the difference?

When God called Abraham in Genesis 12:1–3 he said:

> *"Go from your country, your people and your father's household to the land I will show you. I will make you into a great nation, and I will bless you; I will make your name great, and you will be a blessing. I will bless those who bless you, and whoever curses you I will curse; and all peoples on earth will be blessed through you."*

Here's what we read about God calling Moses in Exodus 3:7–10:

"I have indeed seen the misery of my people in Egypt...So now, go. I am sending you to Pharaoh to bring my people the Israelites out of Egypt."

We observe:

- Abraham was told to leave Harran and begin a journey without a specific destination in mind. God promised to show him along the way. (He knew his general destination was Canaan, but exactly when he knew that and how specific God was deserves further discussion later in this chapter.)

- Abraham was promised territory, blessing, his name to be made great, his descendants to form a nation, and to become the instrument of blessing to everyone on earth.

- Moses was immediately given a specific destination and mission. His assignment? Go to Egypt and tell Pharaoh to release the Israelites and lead them out of the country.

- God promised to be with Moses. God also promised that Moses and the Israelites would worship him on the same mountain where the burning bush encounter took place. (In other words, God promised that the mission would be successful.)

These patriarchs are a study in contrasts: Abraham starts packing his bags while Moses starts making excuses. The reasons Moses gave God for NOT going to Egypt and chatting with Pharaoh?

1. "Who am I? Can't you send someone important?"

2. "I don't even know your name – what if they ask who sent me?"

3. "What if they don't believe me?"

4. "I am not good at speaking in front of groups."

5. "Can't you send someone else? Anyone? Pretty please?"

Moses became the leader of millions because everyone else in line took one step backwards and he never got the text!

No, he didn't want to lead. He tried leading as a younger man, and it was a disaster. He simply wanted to wander the backside of the dessert caring for his father-in-law's sheep.

But, God intervened. God pursued him. Is God intervening in your life? Do you feel pursued? If so, turn towards him. Embrace him. Not only does he have something for you to do, he has someone for you to become along the way. Want to grow into the best possible husband or wife? Submit to God's will and ways and become that person!

A few reflections that are helping us navigate the road before us:

First, both are legitimate calls of God. Moses was reluctant, filled with doubt and fear, and totally unqualified in his own mind. God answered every one of Moses' objections, made provision for him by giving him a staff that morphs into a snake and by sending his brother Aaron to stand with him and communicate to Pharaoh. There are instances when God lays it out for us and explains on the front end what he intends to do and how he intends to do it. He patiently answers our questions and leads us, step by step, into accomplishing his will. Whatever we need he supplies and whatever he supplies is always enough.

Abraham, on the other hand, had a very different experience. His calling was oblique. He was told to leave home and embark on a one-way journey, but several important details were missing. In other words, God left gaps in the revelation. These "God-Gaps" mean that we lack the resources within ourselves to complete the mission and guarantee that if God doesn't show up and fill those gaps we are doomed to failure. (Moses encountered several God-Gaps as well; the primary difference lies in the more detailed revelation he received on the front end and how desperately he tried to excuse himself from the mission.)

Although Abraham's calling was more of a "just-in-time" arrangement, the promises he received were very specific and deeply profound. It was the promise of millions of descendants that captured his heart and imagination. He was an old man with no children, desperate for an heir. If God could make good on this promise leaving home without a GPS would be a small price to pay.

Sandi and I are getting our marching orders from God these days on a "need-to-know" basis. We feel like Israel in the wilderness. We get up each morning, look out of our tent to see if the pillar of cloud stayed put overnight (to determine if we are staying or leaving), and walk outside to collect enough manna for that day. We have no five-year plan. We do not know where we will be living in nineteen months. Our budget is more focused on daily bread than annual forecasts. The marriage retreat we are hosting next month could lead to incredible opportunity or be a complete bust. There is a moment-to-moment texture to our lives; we have climbed out so far on this faith limb there is no turning back. When it eventually snaps we are trusting God to catch us in mid-air.

In this sense we are free.

We are free because we are doing our very best to seek God and his kingdom as our first priority. And the promise he gives us in Matthew 6:33 says that as we do that he will meet all of our needs. So, it's really on him. We need to be faithful with the day-to-day stuff he has asked us to do and trust Him to do all the heavy lifting.

Second, Abrahamic callings tend to develop into Mosaic callings over time. This means that as we are faithful to follow God one day at a time, we will come to a place where he gives us additional revelation (exactly what happened to Abraham). The principle at work: "Be faithful with the little bit of light you have now, and God will shine a brighter light when the time is right." Another way to say it? Stand firmly on the last clear word God gave you.

God is testing and growing our faith. Can we be trusted to obediently take the next step he has clearly shown us (without knowing what lies beyond)? If we can learn what true submission and dependency upon God looks like in that step, he will give us more revelation. Jesus said those who are faithful in small things get entrusted with bigger things...

The danger comes after God gives more revelation and we are tempted to trust the program or strategy more than God. Let's face it, Israel didn't do well after they entered the Promised Land and God gave them detailed revelation on how to live out their daily lives. We see this played out in 1 Samuel 4 as the armies of Israel carry the ark of covenant with them into battle against the Philistines. They trusted the ark of God, but not the God of the ark. The result? 30,000 dead Israelite soldiers on the battlefield, the ark of God captured, and the spiritual leaders of the nation taken out.

The real trick seems to be staying focused on God and not his gifts; to trust the Engineer more than the machine he built. This is one of the reasons we are so passionate about living an UP, IN, and OUT marriage. When we walk by faith and not by sight we grow sensitive to the promptings of his Spirit. Sitting at the feet of Jesus as a normal part of life connects us to his Person. Linking arms with fellow disciples keeps the grace flowing into our lives from the rest of his body. Joining Jesus on his mission keeps us humble and dependent upon him.

It is when we steer clear of the God-Gaps that we become self-reliant, lazy, inward, and small.

We view this next chapter of our lives as a new adventure. We expect God to meet us, guide us, provide for us, and change us. We believe that others will be blessed through the grace he pours onto us. Many details remain to be filled in, but we have already left Harran. Those questions will be answered en route, and that's OK by us...most days.

Third, Abraham was 75 years old when he received his calling in Harran, and Moses was 80.

Think about it.

Some of you feel like it's too late. Many of you think you've missed your chance. A few of you believe you have done something that disqualifies you. And there are those of you who just feel like God has put you on the shelf indefinitely.

How many of us have ever:

- Lied?
- Lost our temper?
- Allowed our fear to put a loved one in harm's way?
- Ran away from our problems instead of facing them?
- Took matters into our own hands when it seemed like God was letting us down?
- Killed a man in anger?

These sins against God and other people are both self-centered and destructive. And they were all committed by Abraham or Moses and recorded in the Bible.

God preserved these accounts on purpose and for a purpose. He wants you and me to know about them.

So, if you think you are too old or too big a sinner for God use you, think again! The big things God wants to do in and through your life lie just beyond your next steps of repentance and obedience. To repent means to change your mind and turn around. To obey means trusting God more than yourself and submitting to His ways of doing things. Obedience is marked by actually doing what God is asking us to do.

One final reflection on this Abrahamic calling: when God called Abraham in Genesis 12 to leave Harran and go to a place he would show him, it wasn't Abraham's first calling. In fact, God called him years before while he was still living in Ur.

We read in Genesis 11:31–32

> *Terah took his son Abram, his grandson Lot son of Haran, and his daughter-in-law Sarai, the wife of his son Abram, and together they set out from Ur of the Chaldeans to go to Canaan. But when they came to Harran, they settled there. Terah lived 205 years, and he died in Harran.*

This passage indicates that God must have called Abraham while he was still living in Ur (modern day Iraq). Not only did he receive his first call while still living in Ur, but God also specified the destination: Canaan. They set out in obedience to God, but for some reason when they reached Harran (modern day Turkey) they settled there. Terah, Abraham's father, dies in Harran. It is only after all this takes place that God appears to Abraham a second time and calls him to leave his new home for Canaan.

This gets confirmed for us in Acts 7: 1–4 in Stephen's defense before the Sanhedrin:

Then the high priest asked Stephen, "Are these charges true?"

To this he replied: "Brothers and fathers, listen to me! The God of glory appeared to our father Abraham while he was still in Mesopotamia, before he lived in Harran. 'Leave your country and your people,' God said, 'and go to the land I will show you.' "So he left the land of the Chaldeans and settled in Harran. After the death of his father, God sent him to this land where you are now living.

So, when our great patriarch was called by God to leave everything behind and go to the land God would show him (so that one day his descendants would become a great nation and bless everyone in the entire world) he obeyed 60%. The journey to Canaan was 1,000 miles, but Abraham only went 600 miles to Harran.

In Harran they settled down, even though they knew God wanted them in Canaan – another 400 miles. Why?

Were they tired? 600 miles in those days was a very long journey. Terah was an old man and Abraham himself was no spring chicken. Maybe they just ran out of gas and figured Harran was far enough.

Were they discouraged? God was asking them to make significant sacrifices, but to what end? Remember, the promises of blessing don't come to Abraham until his second calling in Harran. Did he need a more compelling reason to finish the journey? Was it the promise of Isaac that enabled him to rally his strength and push on?

Did he lose hope? His father was dead, he had no children, and Sarah was past childbearing years. What was the point? The situation certainly looked hopeless. Might as well hunker down and make the best of it.

These are just my speculations; the Bible doesn't say one way or the other. But my guess is that Abraham became content with mostly obeying God while keeping his expectations low.

You ever feel that way?

I have. Many times...

So have a good number of the leaders we coach. And, if you require empirical evidence, look at those statistics we lamented over at the beginning of this chapter again. Just like Abraham and Sarah, we have thousands of leadership couples who have settled in Harran and called it good enough.

No, it isn't the original vision that burned in their hearts when they first got married. Back then they actually believed God had something in store for them; something very different from the reality of the marriage and ministry they now have. Yes, over the years we all have ways of making peace with the disappointment and sadness. After all, we were just kids back then, what did we know?

Right?

But, what if...

What if we had a better handle on God's calling for our marriage in our twenties than we do now? Sure, we were young and inexperienced. Yes, we were naïve about a lot of things. Marriage was a lot easier for most of us before the kids came along, and before that mortgage payment began hitting every month. We can't take those early visions of intimacy and impact too seriously, can we?

Well, I suppose that all depends on our promises. It was the promises of God – unearned, grace-filled, and outrageous – that filled Abraham and Sarah with the faith and strength they needed for a 25-year journey into a strange land and impossible parenthood. Here are two promises we are holding onto as we press into our journey. I offer them to you as stepping-stones for your next chapter.

1. God's promise: We are better together

After 26 years of marriage I am more convinced than ever that it is not good for man to be alone. It is not good for me to be alone. It is not good for Sandi to be alone.

Period.

A sick marriage can be one of the loneliest places on earth; a cold marriage bed is a cruel irony.

I stepped away from our marriage covenant emotionally because I refused to take ownership for my own woundedness (and the destructive strategies I erected to protect myself). Also, I came to believe that my worth was determined by my accomplishments. If Sandi was slowing me down, I needed to move on without her.

Was I better off alone in either of those instances? No, just the opposite.

Isolation is the worst context to deal with past hurts or trauma. We isolate because we don't want anyone to see just how screwed up we really are. We isolate because we push those closest to us away when they touch that tender spot. We isolate because we can't hold onto our coping strategies (that helped us survive at one point) and intimacy at the same time.

It's understandable, but not life giving. I feel empathy for those trapped by it, but it is no less a prison.

Healing comes through transparent, loving, and truth-filled relationships. I needed God's grace in the form of another human being who knew my secrets and loved me in spite of them. I needed someone to say, "I am really sorry your dad wasn't there for you when you were a kid. That must have been really tough." But, I also needed truth. Until I quit blaming my dad or his drinking for my problems I can't grow. I first have to take ownership for the way I am responding to the situation and how that response is harming our marriage. Looking back I know it was my issue, and mine alone. Nothing changed until I owned it.

How about not partnering with Sandi so that I could accomplish more ministry? (It sounds so stupid when I actually write it...) Let's just play this out for a moment:

- The greatest commandment in Scripture is to love God

- The second greatest commandment is to love people

- A husband is told to love his wife sacrificially (the same way Christ loved the church)

- Christian marriage, in fact, is a visual aid to the world for God's love

So, here is the logic: I intend to step away from loving my wife so that I can better show people how loving God is. I choose to disengage from her to better equip leaders to know and implement God's will – the same God that designed marriage for two separate people to become one.

What?

How can any sustainable kingdom advances take place outside of faithful covenant relationships? Impossible.

The real reason I wanted distance from Sandi was my refusal to deal with my own stuff. I had to keep moving quickly onto the next thing fearing people would get too close and see the contradiction in my message and marriage. (Y'all come and be miserable like me! This had to be covered up or compensated for somehow.)

Isolation is a dead end. But, don't be fooled, integration only comes on the far side of an arduous uphill journey.

Some practical ways we are engaging the promise of being better and going farther together?

- We pray together just about every night.

- We prayer walk our neighborhood often.

- We build our family schedule around UP, IN, and OUT.

- We defer to one another with the kids – she is better equipped to lead in certain situations and I am learning to submit to her. She does likewise.

- We meet every Tuesday for lunch to talk over the organizational stuff related to our ministry. Sandi holds my feet to the fire with things I don't want to think about. I am the big picture guy who sees the end goal and builds the strategy to get us from point A to point B. She wants to talk about the details. Even though we frustrate each other at times, we do so much better together.

- We are teaching a marriage class together at church.

- Today we will coach two ministry couples. I will bring the strategy and Sandi will ask good questions, share parts of our story, and pour relational glue onto the conversation. She will also speak her mind on topics she feels strongly about – and the other couples will encounter a woman who has strength to offer.

- We will also talk about our family budget today. We have a lot of big decisions to make about next year and we will make those together.

As you can see, we are going for intense integration. This may be more integration than you want! God may be calling you to other things that require more independent ministry. This must be calibrated for each couple. But one thing is for certain: mutual submission, dying to self, repentance and re-alignment with God's purposes are a must. These won't come cheap or easy. Get ready for a gut-check.

2. God's promise: Happiness in marriage comes through serving one another

Here's how Jesus put it.

- Question: How do you find your life?

    Answer: By losing it.

- Question: How do you lose your life?

    Answer: By clinging to it.

- Question: How do you have a fruitful, fulfilling, abundant life?

    Answer: By dying to yourself.

The life Jesus is talking about (an eternal kind of life) can never be achieved through direct effort. You can't receive eternal life by striving for it, but only through surrender, repentance, and faith. Real life comes after death and resurrection – this is the backbone of Christian theology. Effort is not the currency for the blessed life Jesus speaks of in the Gospels, but absolute trust in God's undeserved grace as your last and only hope. (Effort does come later, but *never* earning.)

I started jogging a few months ago. I am up to 1.6 miles! (Yes, I am *that* good.) I have friends who've run marathons. Let's say I plan to run a marathon in 6 months, what's the best plan?

Well, since I have never run a marathon and never intend to, I can't speak from experience. But, I imagine there would be a training regimen that includes progressively longer runs. I would have to cut back on sweet tea and ice cream. No doubt, consulting a trainer, buying the right gear, and getting more rest would all factor into the equation.

How not to be successful running a marathon? By running a marathon! If I go out tomorrow and attempt to run a marathon, no matter how hard I push myself, I will fail (and probably end up in the ER). The ability to run 26.2 miles comes as a result of a comprehensive training program, not through direct effort.

Happiness in marriage comes through finding your identity and value in Christ, receiving God's grace and truth every day, and serving your spouse from a confident, secure and deeply loved place. Jesus said it is more blessed to give than to receive. Those who look to their spouse to "make them happy" are miserable people. Love, joy, and peace are the fruit of the Spirit (Galatians 5). Fruit is the result of health, nutrition, and fertilization. A tree doesn't produce fruit through direct effort; it's an indirect, organic process.

The fruit of happiness in your marriage will grow from the roots of God's grace, love, and truth. As you humbly share God's love with your spouse, you will discover joy along the way. It's a byproduct. And, it's seasonal. This means it's going to take time for the pruning and growth to eventually produce the fruit you both want. Endurance is essential.

Those who expect their spouse to provide happiness for them in marriage will lose both in the end (happiness and their spouse).

Those who find their life and identity in God will discover ways to meet the needs of their spouse as good fruit grows from the good soil of their hearts.

And so, Sandi and I cling to our Abrahamic calling. Our faith in his promises of going farther as a team, and finding joy along the way sustains us. The vision of being blessed to be a blessing energizes us.

What about you?

Where do you go from here? Some of you feel adrift in that deep, dark water clinging to the wreckage afloat around you. To you we say:

1. HOLD ON! Do whatever you can to stay afloat.

2. Get help. Some would rather see their marriage die than admit they are wrong or need help. Don't be that foolish. We are so grateful to the pastors and Christian counselors who walked with us through our darkest days. If you don't know what Christian counseling involves or where to find a good Christian counselor check out this website: www.cloudtownsend.com /resources/counselor

3. Own your contribution. Even if you have only made a 1% contribution to the problem, own it, confess it, and

seek forgiveness. You can't change or control your spouse – so start with yourself.

If you believe your marriage is in crisis and heading toward divorce, please do something about it now. There is help available for you that has literally saved thousands of terminally ill marriages. A good starting point is www.hopeformarriages.com.

To all of you who want real-life, practical help in building a marriage on mission we recommend:

1. Pray for a healthy couple who live UP, IN, and OUT together and invite them over for a meal. Share your hearts with them and ask them if they would consider mentoring you. (Models trump strategy every time – IF you can gain accessibility.) Plan to connect with them at least once a month and observe their marriage and way of life. Ask good questions and find out how they build covenant while serving kingdom purposes.

2. Take one idea from this book (maybe walking together or praying before bed) and just start doing it. If you are the one reading this book then you need take initiative. Ask your spouse if they will follow you – don't nag or manipulate.

3. Get your calendar out and talk about what UP, IN, and OUT might look like by repurposing things you are already doing – not by adding new things. Starting with UP, repurpose a meal, bedtime routine, or whatever. Once that becomes a habit (about 6 weeks) repeat the process for IN and OUT.

Another option would be to seek out a coaching relationship. There are good Christian coaches out there, and some focus on working with couples. If we can be of any help go to www.marriageonmission.com to see what we offer (if nothing else we can point you in the right direction).

James warns us against just hearing God's word, but not doing something about it. Is God speaking to you right now? If so, be a doer! Make a commitment today to take one practical next step and share that commitment with a friend who will lovingly hold you accountable.

From Sandi

Thankfully the story of my marriage is not finished and God is still working on me. I wish I could say, "I used to struggle with this in my marriage, now I don't...God is good". I'm telling you that I am a work in progress. Sometimes I make mistakes, and my story looks ugly...and God is still good. In many ways, writing this book has been difficult because it means I can't pretend that everything is okay all the time. I can't hide and say that my weaknesses don't exist. Tom and I are both sinners who bring our baggage into the relationship. It is true that we have been saved by grace, the old is gone and the new has come. We are new creatures in Christ who have everything we need for life and godliness...but we are not perfect. I can't put our story in a box and tie it up with a pretty red bow. This is not the perfect marriage book with all the answers. It is our story. Life happens. It is good and it is hard and it keeps on going.

There is still so much that I don't know.

I don't need to earn my worth as a person or as a wife. I am not defined by my failures or my successes. I need to courageously cling to faith and the God who gives me life. God is the reason I have hope and strength and a voice to share the lessons learned in my marriage.

I do know a few things.

I know that Jesus loves me and is with me through it all. I hold steadfast to the truth that God is good. Based on that,

I am capable.

Philippians 4:13 *"I can do all things through Christ who strengthens me."* (NKJV)

God is my father and my identity is secure as His precious daughter. God has forgiven me, empowered me, and through Christ I am a capable partner. These are true statements even when I don't feel it or act like it. It is helpful for me to proclaim **whose** I am to live out **who** I am.

This journey is not for my husband to travel alone. This is a partnership and I am all in. I wake up each day, look at the cloud, collect the manna, and get to work. Today I am contacting a few churches to see about scheduling speaking events, workshops, and retreats. I'm honestly not sure how next year will turn out or how God will provide, but I trust that He will.

Until Tom and I get different marching orders from God, I will keep pressing into this Marriage on Mission ministry. While the specifics are not always clear, right now I know that God brought me to South Carolina to pursue ministry partnership with Tom. If an opportunity or activity doesn't fit into that calling, then I know to reject it. Right now this is my lens for making decisions.

Tom and I went for a walk yesterday and talked about the future. We talked about church and life and we prayed while we walked. The conversation didn't feel forced or stressed, just natural. For me this is something to celebrate and I am thankful to see the progress we have made. This was a good day and God is good. God is still good even if tomorrow is difficult. The point is this; I'm accepting that my life and marriage is a journey of faith. There's no pressure to be perfect. Maybe my imperfect story will encourage you to take steps in faith and avoid some mistakes.

Maybe it will make you realize that there is hope for your marriage, regardless of how you are feeling right now. Hopefully it will encourage you to submit to God and his plan for your life. Jesus really does love you. After all, that is really what it is all about.

Conclusion:
Where We Go From Here...

Sandi and I finished writing this book about a month ago. Since then we have done our best to get the word out, asked several friends to read the manuscript and give input, and worked on a hundred details related to the publishing process.

However, those weren't the most important things. Let me tell you about the real progress we've made over the past thirty days.

First, I reached out to a few men I know from church and asked them to meet me for breakfast. Between bites of bacon and toast loaded with strawberry jam (the most important part of any breakfast) I asked them a question:

"Will you join me on a journey to live a life worth imitating and pursue a marriage on mission?"

I asked three men this question, and they have all initially agreed. In fact, I meet with two of them tomorrow morning to actually engage the process. What will the process look like? That remains to be seen, but I am confident it will include the following elements:

1. We will agree upon a day and time to meet every week and make every effort to show up.

2. We will agree upon a Bible reading plan and discuss how God is speaking to us through his word.

3. We will ask one another certain accountability questions every week, answer them honestly, confess our sin to one another, and celebrate the victories. These questions will touch areas of our lives like sexual purity, our pursuit of God and our spouse, and our witness to a lost world.

4. We will pray for one another.

That's pretty much it. Our group will get no larger than four men and our meetings will last no longer than 60–90 minutes. If God brings a fifth guy into our group, we will become two groups.

You may be wondering why I am writing about a men's discipleship idea in a book about marriage. Here's the deal: If I intend to serve, lead, and engage Sandi in a growing marriage on mission I will need a support system outside of our relationship.

Remember, only two whole people can become one. Sandi's job is not to complete me, her job is to help and partner with me in discovering and living out God's will. If I look only to her for all of my emotional, friendship, and personal needs to be met I am setting both of us up for failure. God meets all of my needs, and he does so through relationships. It just so happens he chooses to meet some of those needs through friendships with other guys – and it's my responsibility to cultivate those relationships and bring that health into my marriage.

Sandi is seeking out healthy relationships with a few other women as well. Yesterday she walked with Michele and today she had lunch with Joyce. I am striving to grow into a good husband, but I will never make a wonderful girlfriend. She needs both, and so do I.

The principle: Build a support system outside of your marriage with safe, same sex friends who know you and love you. Instead of pressuring your mate to become all things for you, bring the strength you glean from those friendships into your marriage to better serve and bless your spouse.

There is grace and challenge I receive from my brothers in Christ that I can get nowhere else. This is why we must ultimately look beyond marriage on mission to family on mission – our marriages must be nourished from the rich soil of Christian community.

Second, we had a big fight a few weeks ago. In fact, it was on the same day we completed the first draft of this book. It wasn't a long argument, but what it lacked in duration it more than compensated for with intensity.

Come to think of it, we tussled again this morning.

Why am I telling you this?

We are sold out for all God wants to do in and through our marriage – this is real life for us. However, we are also committed to wrestling through every disappointment and setback. We have been reminded in the past three weeks that progress for us looks like two steps forward, and one step back.

The reason for some of the struggles of late has been my lack of engagement (I blame my travel schedule, but that's not entirely true) and not enough walking together. Our walks function like a pressure release valve, and if we miss that communication it's only a matter of time before something explodes. So, this afternoon we are taking a long walk and I will intentionally engage in the things she needs to talk about. I have a few stresses weighing on my heart that need to be ventilated as well. (These anxieties have taken up so much emotional bandwidth for me I have withdrawn into myself – the very impulse I need to resist.)

The principle: Insist upon consistent communication patterns that make room for venting, dreaming, and processing loss. (When you blow-up, give grace, seek forgiveness, and get back into healthy communication rhythms.)

And last, don't lose sight of the mission! I have struggled with my OUT relationships this month. So many other things have gotten in the way (again, several excuses come to mind – there is a never ending stream). Our last Saturday brunch was over six weeks ago, and prayer walking has been pretty anemic since then. I knew in my heart today that we needed to pray and look for opportunity.

We made three decisions this afternoon.

1. Our date night tonight (both kids are gone) will be baking chocolate chip cookies and preparing gift bags for ten neighbors with Christmas cookies and an invitation to brunch this Saturday. (Sandi made me promise I would stay in the kitchen at her side until the job was done – I agreed as long as she promised I could eat as many cookies as I want.)

2. I will cancel my duck-hunting trip for Saturday and we will hold a neighborhood brunch. (Don't be too impressed by my spiritual fervor, getting up at 4 a.m. sounds less and less appealing as I get older.)

3. We are going to visit a neighbor who is holding church services in her home. We saw the yard signs over a month ago – and we both believe God wants us to get to know this family and see if there may be some ways we can partner together to make the good news of Jesus tangible to our neighbors.

So, there it is! Not very glamorous, is it? Like I said, this is real life – and real life gets messy. One minute you are writing a book about ministry partnership, and the next you are yelling at one another. Not sure we will ever fully outgrow the back and forth nature of this. Not sure we are supposed to this side of heaven...

We leave you with this encouragement:

"...surely I am with you always, to the very end of the age."

~ Jesus, Matthew 28:20

You may have huge obstacles to overcome, but you are not alone. And, where there is Jesus there is hope.

Acknowledgements

Sandi and I wish to express our appreciation to those who made this book possible.

We want to thank our friend and publisher, Dave DeVries. You have been with us from the first day and have guided our every step. Your constant encouragement and gentle nudges kept us moving forward.

To our friend and editor, Doug Connelly - thank you. Your mentorship helped us to believe we had something worth saying. Your practical help through the editing process made this a much better book.

We thank the leadership of Pawleys Island Community Church. You provided a quiet place for us to write when life was too hectic at home. Thank you also for donating space for our first marriage retreat.

Sandi wants to specifically thank the ladies of "The Dana Table" (you know who you are!). You provided a safe place to process and grow.

To Greg Houseman and Jim Keller - you have been like brothers to me and your friendship has made me a better man in every respect.

- Tom and Sandi Blaylock

About Tom and Sandi Blaylock

Tom and Sandi coach ministry couples, travel to churches to teach marriage on mission principles, and conduct marriage workshops and retreats. Tom serves nationally as a leadership coach and trainer. They have three children and live in South Carolina.

They would love to partner with you or your church. Contact them today at: www.marriageonmission.com